Nobody's Child

A Generation Caught in the Middle

Kaleidoscope

Statement of Purpose

Kaleidoscope is a series of adult educational resources developed for the ecumenical church by Lancaster Theological Seminary and the United Church Board for Homeland Ministries. Developed for adults who want serious study and dialogue on contemporary issues of Christian faith and life, Kaleidoscope offers elective resources designed to provide new knowledge and new understanding for persons who seek personal growth and a deeper sense of social responsibility in their lives.

Kaleidoscope utilizes the expertise of professionals in various disciplines to develop study resources in both print and video. The series also provides tools to help persons develop skills in studying, reflecting, inquiring critically, and exploring avenues of appropriate Christian responses in life.

Kaleidoscope provides sound and tested resources in theology, biblical studies, ethics, and other related subjects that link personal growth and social responsibility to life situations in which adult Christian persons develop.

Nobody's Child
A Generation Caught in the Middle

Paul E. Irion

A Kaleidoscope Series Resource

United Church Press
New York

To struggling parents and children of all ages.

"The web of our life is of a mingled yarn, good and ill together."

Shakespeare, *All's Well that Ends Well*, iv 3.

KALEIDOSCOPE SERIES

Copyright © 1989 by United Church Press

All rights reserved

No part of this publication may be reproduced, stored in a retrieval system, or transmitted in any form or by any means—electronic, mechanical, photocopying, recording, or otherwise (brief quotations used in magazine or newspaper reviews excepted)—without the prior permission of the publisher.

All scripture quotations, unless otherwise indicated, are from the Revised Standard Version of the Bible, copyrighted 1946, 1952, © 1971, 1973, by the Division of Christian Education of the National Council of Churches of Christ in the United States of America, and are used by permission. Additional acknowledgment of permissions are found in the Notes section of this volume.

Library of Congress Cataloging-in-Publication Data

Irion, Paul E.
  Nobody's child : a generation caught in the middle / Paul E. Irion.
  —(Kaleidoscope)
  Bibliography: p. 101
  ISBN 0-8298-0813-2.   —ISBN 0-8298-0814-0 (leader's guide ed.)
  1. Middle aged persons—United States—Psychology. 2. Adult education—United States—Family relationships. 3. Intergenerational relations—United States. 4. Life cycle, Human—Religious aspects—Christianity.
5. Family—Religious aspects—Christianity. I. Title. II. Series: Kaleidoscope (Lancaster Theological Seminary (Lancaster, Pa.))
HQ1059.4.174   1989
155.6'6—dc20   89-4819

United Church Press, 132 West 31 Street, New York, NY 10001

Contents

Kaleidoscope: Statement of Purpose	ii
Introduction to the Kaleidoscope Series	vii
1. The Years in the Middle	1
2. Examining Our Assumptions	11
3. A Values Crunch with the Younger Generation	27
4. The Empty Nest Revisited	43
5. Caring for the Older Generation	59
6. Confronting the Death of the Older Generation	77
Postscript	96
Notes	97
Bibliography	101

Introduction to the Kaleidoscope Series

Through direct experience, our faculty at Lancaster Theological Seminary discovered that a continual demand exists for Christian theological reflection upon issues of current interest. To meet this demand, the Seminary for many years has offered courses for lay people. To offer the substance of these courses to the wider Christian public is the purpose of the Kaleidoscope Series.

Lancaster Seminary exists to proclaim the gospel of Jesus Christ for the sake of the church and the world. In addition to preparing men and women for the ordained Christian ministry, the Seminary seeks to be a center of theological reflection for clergy and laity. Continuing education and leadership development for all Christians focus our mission. The topics and educational style in the Kaleidoscope Series extend Lancaster Seminary's commitment: theological study reflective of the interaction of the Bible, the world, the church, worship, and personal faith. We hope that this course will provide an opportunity for you to grow in self-understanding, in knowledge of other people and God's creation, and in the spirit of Christ.

We wish to thank the staff of the Division of Education and Publication of the United Church Board for Homeland Ministries for their leadership in this enterprise. The Rev. Dr. Ansley Coe Throckmorton, The Rev. Dr. Larry E. Kalp, and The Rev. Dr. Percel E. Alston provided encouragement and support for the project. In particular, we are grateful for the inspiration of Percel Alston, who was a trustee of Lancaster Seminary. His life-long interest in adult education makes it most appropriate that this series be dedicated to him. Three other staff members have guided the series through the writing and production stages: The Rev. Jack H. Haney, Project Coordinator for the Kaleidoscope Series, The Rev. Nancy G. Wright, Editor for Kaleidoscope, and Mr. Gene Permé, Marketing Director. As a publishing staff they have provided valuable experience and counsel. Finally, I wish to recognize the creative leadership of Mrs. Jean Vieth, the Seminary Coordinator for the Series, who has been active for several years in this educational program at Lancaster.

Peter M. Schmiechen, President
The Lancaster Theological Seminary

Chapter 1

The Years in the Middle

The experience of mid-life has many dimensions. These include the whole developmental process of the middle years—the growth of the self—examined in light of the "passages" about which Gail Sheehey wrote so well. Valuable as that analysis is, this volume will take another perspective: the intergenerational pressures felt by so many middle-aged people.

Being Middle Aged

Some people find approaching middle age a fearful prospect. Our culture puts so heavy an emphasis on youth and early adulthood that many of us feel reluctant to tell our age; some of us even spend a great deal of time trying to look younger than we really are. We are dubious about the adage that "Life begins at forty"; we may see entry into the middle years more as the beginning of a long, slow decline that ends in dying than as a prelude to new life. And those thoughts do not sit well with us.

Well-versed in the ways in which early childhood and parenting influence the development of identity, we may assume that all significant personal development takes place in childhood and adolescence. Adulthood, correspondingly, is viewed as developmentally static. Just as we do not continue to grow taller, we are not inclined to look upon middle age as a time for significant personal growth.

However, adulthood is the longest developmental stage (four to five decades for many people). Because many years are involved and the developmental steps occur gradually, we may not notice them. Lillian E. Troll points out three kinds of development that occur within each person: (1) the familiar developmental stages that take place within the person's life span; (2) development within a family context as a person moves from one generation to another in the family structure, from the younger to the older generations; (3) development within what sociologists call "age cohorts"—those people in the same generation in a society.[1]

An example of age cohorts is the generation of persons who lived through World War I as children and were late adolescents or young adults during the Great Depression. Most had only a high school education; many of the men were in military service in World War II; some of the women worked in industry. While this cohort experienced a rising standard of living in post-war prosperity, they never forgot the depression; consequently, economic security holds a place of high importance.

Those who are presently middle-aged experienced childhood during the depression. Men and women of this cohort carried the major burdens of World War II in both the military and industry. The GI bill enabled many to go to college and graduate school; many women returned to traditional homemaker roles after war work. They are the babyboom parents. For many of them, post-war prosperity enabled home ownership, moves to the suburbs, relative affluence, and a comfortable life-style. These parents are now at, or just past, the peak of their careers. The 1960s counterculture, marked by rebellion, drugs, and the sexual revolution, attracted many of their children, creating high parental anxiety. Their own parents are now quite old or are dying.

The cohort who are at present younger adults grew up in postwar affluence. Large numbers went to college as a matter of course, supported by their parents. Quite early they married and had children. Although many had varying degrees of exposure to the counterculture of the 1960s, most took the affluence of their parents for granted, moving beyond it into their own "yuppie-dom."

The second cohort described above, the middle-aged, find themselves in a time of assessment. They evaluate themselves as persons and as parents. This evaluation produces a vulnerability for the sensitive person in middle years. It leads to questions such as, "Could I have done better as a parent?" and "Have I achieved as much of my potential as I should?" The ultimate dimension of their vulnerability rests in the growing awareness of mortality, an awareness that can stimulate a new seriousness about living. Thus, the middle-years' assessment can be occasion for deep development and growth.[2]

The Intergenerational Network

Focusing on the intergenerational network in middle age complements the understanding of individual personal development of middle-aged persons. Holding together the two perspectives—individual and network—provides a true and useful picture.

Persons exist as unique beings: individuality is an essential mark of personhood. A sense of personal identity, that which makes me ME, is an absolute necessity. But a person in isolation is anomalous. We become who we are as persons in a network of relationships. Many times this complex network, in which we live and work, is called a system. Our heavy cultural emphasis on individualism may occasion our missing this systems understanding. In contrast, the ancient Hebrews conceptualized persons as meaningful parts of the larger community of Israel. They understood that the order of creation mandated the human life lived in community.

A system reflects more than a collection of component parts. For example, let us think of the family as a system, our own family, the one in which we grew up. Most of us lived in a matrix of one or usually two parents and one or more siblings, each a unique person interacting with all the other family members—interdependent. But we also knew that our family had an identity of its own. That family system developed into something more than the sum total of its individual members. This sense of being a family contributed to who we were and who we have become.

We never fully leave our families, even though we depart from the homes in which we grew up. Therefore, the better we understand our family relationships and the way in which the family as a community has affected our development, the better we will understand ourselves.

Although growing up in a family of two-generations, we lived in a context that involved also the influences of prior generations. We know how we are related to other family members and have feelings about many of these relationships. It is important to realize that through past years our feelings about these relationships have had a profound effect on their present shape. So the family system affects both the rational and the emotional sides of our experience of selfhood. The family systems model gives help in understanding the inter-generational dimensions of all of our lives and particularly of middle-aged people.

Dynamics Within the Family System of the Middle Aged

This study focuses on three generations: young adult children, middle-aged parents, and the latter's elderly parents. The relationships among these three generations can be very positive and constructive, expressive of the continuity of a family and the passing of wisdom and strength from one generation to another. These relationships may also involve tensions, struggles for power, conflicts of interest, and competition for resources. Just as in any relationship an inevitable pull exists between the interest of self and the interest of others, so within any family system these interests exert pressure on members, requiring an effort to maintain a balance in the family.

An exploration of intergenerational pressures is important. Even when such pressures are not part of a family's experiences, exploration of them can create sensitivity to others who may be living through them. Because these tensions are considered here from within the context of the church, we can learn to empathize with the pains and sorrows of each other as friends in the faith and become alert to ways in which the church can minister to those with such needs.

The title of this book is *Nobody's Child*. Originally this term was used to describe a middle-aged person grieving the death of the last surviving parent. The title also paints a picture of a number of other situations, touched upon in this book. In a sense the late adolescent or young adult, in the normal developmental struggle for autonomy and identity, comes to feel that he or she is nobody's child. The sheltered, dependent status of "child" is being relegated to the past. Because the parents of most elderly persons have died, the elderly have long since been nobody's child. But now, faced with uncertain circumstances, they may resume some of the dependencies of childhood. Meanwhile, their middle-aged cildren are struggling with the ambiguities of becoming their surrogate parents, another form of being nobody's child.

For some the circumstances of such tensions are dramatic and highly charged. For others the adjustments required by the dynamic flow of generational need and resources in a family system may be minimal. In every instance, however, the family cannot escape a meeting with these issues.

Modes of Relating Within the Family System

Our study focuses on three modes of relating within the family system: dependence, independence, and interdependence. These terms refer to three distinct ways of balancing needs and resources.

Dependence involves two persons: one who has a need and another with resources. Clearly, they do not relate as equals, because the person with a need feels vulnerable, while the person with the needed resources has power over the other. Dependency can be either developmental or the result of a crisis situation. It is necessary and inevitable that little children be dependent, for example, but for others, life situations or crises may cause dependency, temporary or chronic. We all experience moments when we have to depend upon another person for help. However, some people adopt a characteristic pattern, a life-style, of leaning on someone else.

Independence, a position of strength, takes its place at the other end of the continuum. A person who is independent perceives that he or she has resources sufficient to meet personal needs. Although independence is never absolute, because a healthy existence does not permit that kind of total isolation, our culture places high value on independence, both politically and personally. We give positive strokes to the person who is self-sufficient, who can "stand on his or her own feet," who does not need to call regularly on the resources of others.

The third mode is interdependence. Interdependence implies that people have differing gifts to contribute to the whole family system. *Each person both gives and receives.* The balancing of needs and resources is not just an individual matter. Rather, the family unit, as a system, provides the foundation for meeting needs that occur within it. It is like the metaphor Saint Paul uses to describe the church: one body with many members, each making a unique contribution.[3]

This organismic metaphor, one body with many members, suggests not only cooperation and mutuality but also the uniqueness of each member. Not only are the members bound together but they also retain their own freedom to be themselves. A person's unique function is like the hand that needs the eye in order to guide it and the eye that needs the hand to touch what it perceives.

Interdependence does not negate either dependence or independence. A person can be dependent or independent within an interdependent relationship, so long as that dependence or independence is developmentally or situationally appropriate. At times mutuality has to be adjusted to a limited contribution on the part of one of the members, for example, a very young child or a very frail elderly person. In a sense then, the potential for development constitutes the infant's contribution, while the memory of past accomplishment serves as sufficient offering on the part of the failing elderly. Interdependence fuels a dynamic system, balancing, changing, adjusting, and adapting as needs and resources change.

The Shifting Balance of Need and Resource

A fascinating process called homeostasis operates constantly in each of our bodies. Health requires that many different balances be maintained in our bodies. These assure the proper quantity of water, sodium, potassium, and other minerals. Our bodies are filled with water stored in tissues. This water regulates our body temperature, lubricates our joints, is the medium for biochemical changes, and maintains the proper amount of blood in our circulatory system. The process of homeostasis keeps our water content relatively constant. When heavy perspiration reduces our internal water supply and our salivary glands dry up, we become thirsty and drink. If we drink more than our body requires, we eliminate the excess. Homeostasis involves both continuity and change; it works for stability without being static. We know that our water content is constantly changing, but homeostasis constantly brings it back to a healthy level.

Homeostasis, which is a purely physical process, can also be thought of in psychological and social terms. "Homeostasis" can function in a family system, balancing the resources of the individuals to the needs within the system. Sometimes the process functions in a particular person; sometimes it is seen in the interdependence of persons or generations.

Troll points out:

> The middle generation (parents of married children) is the lineage bridge between the older and the younger generations, helping both and involved with both. Each generation turns to the kinship network for the help it needs: grandparents for care in illness and household management, middle-aged parents for emotional gratification, and young marrieds for assistance with finances and child care.[4]

An article by Markides and others reports studies showing that the middle-aged generation provides the most help in the family system, being heavily relied upon by their children and their aging parents.[5] Even though they receive as well, they are the primary givers in the three-generational system.

Normally a good deal of give and take, interdependence, exists between family members. If a difficulty or special need arises for one member, the others are also affected. Ideally, the whole system will respond. Some of these special needs, like paying college tuition, develop predictably as a person moves up the generational ladder. A crisis precipitates other needs: loss of a job, divorce, serious illness, death of a spouse.

Social Influences in Balancing Need and Resource

As mentioned earlier, western society places very high value upon individualism and personal freedom. This means that our society encourages children to develop independence during adolescence and young adulthood. It increasingly (albeit somewhat unevenly) supports equality for men and women in the family, makes the nuclear family a necessity for many, and simultaneously provides financial resources for many elderly.

A great deal of interdependence characterized agrarian families of past generations. The combination of mobility, urbanization, division of labor into specialties, and relative affluence has broken that pattern. For example, your sweater today is not knitted by your grandmother but by an unseen machine operatior in Korea or Taiwan. This, too, reflects interdependence, but on a global scale, and is much more difficult to appreciate sensitively.

Increased longevity in our time also has had a major impact on changes in the balance of a person's needs and resources. Demographers tell us that in less than fifty years the number of people over sixty-five years of age in the United States will be one and a half times the sixty-five million now in that category. We are becoming increasingly aware of the strains the growth in the elderly population may put on social and family resources to provide for people in the later years of life.

Responding to the Shifting Balance of Need

In the homeostatic process in our bodies the balance of water content constantly shifts. We drink fluid, we perspire, we eliminate. The process of bringing our bodies back into balance is so efficient that we do not even notice it. But on occasion the disequilibrium has dramatic manifestations: a person sweats through an hour of lawn mowing or a vigorous tennis game, or someone with heart problems experiences a buildup of fluid in the ankles. These imbalances call for more aggressive responses: several cool drinks or a prescribed diuretic.

The balancing process in the relationships among generations also functions automatically most of the time. But special urgent needs occur, requiring more than ordinary reaction in order to restore the family's balance. As a prelude to our consideration of specific situations, the following section explains some general patterns of reaction that people have to situations of disequilibrium.

Victimized by the Imbalance of Needs and Resources

A crisis in a family system affects all its members. However, reactions differ. One group of people respond to another's need in a helpful way but feel victimized by the circumstances or by the person in need. This situation creates a form of dependency, not only in the person with the crucial need, but also in those being depended upon. Because they, too, feel caught in the web of the other's need, their response is motivated by a sense of obligation, sometimes joyless.

Counter-productively, such a sense of victimization produces frustration, anger, guilt, and a lack of self-actualization for both giver and receiver. An extended period of need often produces this kind of response. While the initial response of the person with resources is positive, as time passes and the need continues indefinitely, his or her sense of being victimized grows.

We must recognize that at times a potential caregiver is genuinely victimized, imposed upon by a family member who is inappropriately or pathologically dependent. One suffers as a victim when called upon to help another, if that person can help himself or herself but refuses to do so.

Resisting Responding to the Imbalance

For people victimized by the inappropriate or pathological requirements of others, Eda LeShan strongly urges the response pattern expressed in the phrase, "I resist!"[6] She favorably compares adolescence and middle age as two optimum times for making great strides in the development of selfhood. She sees what she calls "middlescence" as a time in which a person has new freedom from the responsibilities of earlier adulthood, while simultaneously working under the sense of urgency provided by the recognition that a lifetime is not endless.

She urges middle-aged persons to seize the opportunity to develop and to resist hindrances to that process. When an older or younger person tries to lay claim on the time or resources of the middle-aged, LeShan writes: "I want to go on caring and loving; I feel compassion and empathy for the struggles of those who are older and younger—but I am also thinking more and more of what I need for my own sense of being most alive and growing."[7]

LeShan feels that it is good to encourage people to accept responsibility for their own needs and to resist pressure to assume "parental" responsibility for their parents. While it is not clear whether she is speaking of parents in truly desperate situations or those who are emotionally dependent but who could take care of themselves if they really tried, she writes: "We may have to learn to live with some feelings of guilt for not satisfying the endless needs of parents, relatives, friends, co-workers, but if ever there is a time to say, 'I am for *me*,' it is in middle age."[8]

LaShan's approach seems to be largely individualistic rather than a family systems approach. Her deep concern is that people stand on their own rather than as members of an interdependent network. It will be interesting and helpful for you to think through what in LeShan's approach you can affirm and what you would like to question. Or do you see these two responses—being victimized, or resisting by insisting on your own right to independence—as extreme statements of the options? Are there yet other ways in which middle-aged persons respond to needs that arise in their family situations?

The Church Reflects on Changes in Balance

The Judeo-Christian tradition acknowledges the oneness of humanity as part of creation, with all persons linked together in the human system despite their obvious diversity. This tradition affirms human beings as essentially interdependent, and caring for the needs of others as the desired life-style. However, one person is not to dominate another in a dependent situation; with each person sharing his or her own gifts, mutuality is the norm for relationship.

Furthermore, biblical tradition regards creation as dynamic, unfinished, changing. The church's vision holds up a future that grows out of the present. Existence moves toward a greater fulfillment of potential, so to stand still, changeless, is to live counter to God's realm. This dynamic quality in all of life enables hope. Contrarily, to feel locked into a static pattern, unable to effect positive change, engenders despair.

Intergenerational relationships within a family provide a context in which we grapple with life's meaning. Because the struggle to affirm meaning is a spiritual endeavor, it is a proper concern for the church. As we look in future chapters at experiences of some middle-aged people, that dramatically effect disequilibrium in their lives, we will include discussion of ways in which the church can participate as a pastoral caregiver.

The word "pastoral" should not be thought of as simply describing the work of the pastor. Rather, it gives expression to the function of the entire church, alluded to in a wonderful ancient metaphor: shepherding. As an image, shepherding may summon up bearded men in flowing robes, carrying crooks and little lambs, in another age from computers, jets, and television. Nevertheless, the metaphor can convey its root meaning: caring, nurturing, protecting, and guiding.

Pastoral caring in this book means the work of the entire church through education, group support and fellowship, worship, service, advocacy for the vulnerable, and counseling. Its activity weaves the church into a network of interdependence, where both the weak and the strong bear one another's burdens.

Chapter 2

Examining Our Assumptions for Dealing with Intergenerational Issues

We do not confront the issues that face middle-aged persons who relate to young adult children and elderly parents in a valueless vacuum. Our faith community and our society provide us with a number of presuppositions about how these issues should be resolved. But these presuppositions cannot to be accepted uncritically; they offer guidelines that we must carefully think through as we struggle to do what we believe is best.

Assumptions Growing Out of Our Religious Heritage

Assumption 1. It is difficult to understand the biblical view of the family as presenting a single, normative pattern valid for all times.

Although some people glibly refer to "the biblical view of marriage and family," this presents a very elusive concept. Because the Bible records the experiences of people and nations, it contains many family pictures that are not all alike. Rather, they show a variety of complex and diverse models of family living.

There are both polygamous and monogamous families. Many biblical family models are strongly patriarchal. A great deal of power resides in the father; often mothers and daughters are regarded as property. Inheritance patterns give all the father's property to the eldest son.

In the teachings of Jesus the affirmation of mutual love and caring illuminates the basis of family life, but Jesus also asserts that the claims of discipleship outweigh the claims of family responsibility. While the teachings of the early church on family life, contained in scattered passages throughout the New Testament epistles, give attention to love, caring, and regard, they also reveal the submission and obedience that was implied in the Old Testament patriarchal model. Procreation was a goal of marriage. Children assured the future in both figurative and practical ways; the continuity of the tribe conferred a kind of personal immortality. Hence, the birth of each new generation was extremely important.

Ancient Hebrew society provided that a childless widow be married to and impregnated by her deceased husband's elder brother so that she would not go through her life without family and children. In the extended family model, children provided social security, for theirs was the responsibility of caring for elderly parents. In a low population agrarian society a large number of children were an economic asset because their hands meant that more work could be done. In such a society interdependence weaves a major theme.

Only a few brief scriptural passages could be described as teachings about family life and about relationships between the generations. This has posed a problem for the church. Christians regard the Bible as a norm for faith and morals, but the fragmentary and sometimes contradictory nature of the family pictures in the Bible make this normative use very difficult. The most obvious illustration of this difficulty is the adoption of monogamy as the normative form for marriage and the laying aside of all the models of polygamous families.

The problems become more troublesome around other complex relational family issues. For example, on the basis of the biblical teachings that follow the patriarchal model, some people in our time resist the idea of equality in the roles of husband and wife and endorse a dominant role for the man and a submissive role for the woman. They clearly adopt the patriarchal family as normative, over contemporary desires for a more democratic and participatory family.

The questions then become, "How authoritative is the Bible in presenting norms for family life?" and "How does one interpret and use the variety of family pictures in scripture?" We can readily see that the configuration of family life in our time corresponds to our era's social realities: urbanized living, industrialization, democracy, employment of large numbers of women outside the home, public schools, Social Security, and so on. Undoubtedly the biblical pictures show families that were shaped by the social realities of their day: a nomadic or agrarian society; labor-intensive household activities—food gathering and preparation, weaving and sewing; monarchy; rudimentary measures for the social assistance of the needy from outside the family—gleaning, limited charity to widows and orphans; and so forth. The social realities of the two cultures differ so much that it is difficult to find a single normative family model.

There are two basic stances for understanding how the Bible can be normative for our twentieth-century living. One is to insist that the Bible presents an unchangeable truth absolutely separate from the ways in which human society has changed throughout the centuries. The other is to hold that many descriptions of human attitudes and behavior in scripture reflect the cultural milieu of that generation and have to be reinterpreted to have meaning in the present time.

The problem is that both of these positions hold some truth. There are some elements of the teaching of the Bible as applicable now as twenty-five centuries ago. For example, scripture confers high value on love with no strings attached: God's love for all creation, family love, love for enemies. On the other hand, just as we do not feel obligated to trade in our democratic government for a biblical monarchy, so we do not need to feel bound to patriarchal family relationships. To regard the Bible as a norm for our living requires that we be able to draw a line of understanding between these two kinds of interpretation. Herbert Anderson sums up the issue this way:

> We take the Bible seriously when we regard it as a historical document which is itself constantly involved in a struggle to express God's care for the world. It is inevitable, though, that forms of family care change over the years because they are as much responsive to human need as they are reflective of the enduring nature of God.[1]

The question then becomes, "What changes and what does not?" Christians may affirm basic attitudes, such as mutual love given without conditions, desire for mutual growth in grace, and care for the weak and vulnerable, as enduring norms for family living. Yet the forms in which we live out these norms will be variously molded by cultural conditions. Changing greatly across the years, no one form can be regarded as everlasting. Rather, the form taken by family life in any generation is best understood as a creative possibility, an opportunity to try anew to live out in families the enduring biblical values of mutual love and caring.

Assumption 2. The commandment "Honor your father and mother" does not simply establish the authority of middle-aged parents and require the support of elderly parents but supports interdependence.

Part of the family pictures in the Bible shows the scriptural understanding of intergenerational relations. Basic to this understanding in Judeo-Christian tradition is the Fifth Commandment: "Honor your father and your mother, as the Lord your God commanded you; that your days may be prolonged, and that it may go well with you, in the land which the Lord your God gives you."[2]

The focus of the commandment is not simply kindly treatment of parents or the sanctioning of their authority. The outcome of the commandment confers benefit on the child (of whatever age) of these parents: "that your days may be prolonged, and that it may go well with you." The commandment does not strike a bargain, that is, "If you look after your parents, you'll get a long, happy life in return." Rather, the consequence of keeping this commandment is that the social fabric is strengthened and life is better for everyone. Here, everyone's needs are cared for; one generation passes values to another, enabling a good life. This commandment, by focusing on the benefits to children, draws a picture of interdependence.

The teachings of Jesus frequently offer broader or more challenging interpretations of many of the commandments, including the Fifth Commandment. Matthew 15 and Mark 7 record accounts of Jesus applying this commandment to elders of the religious community, not simply to biological parents.[3] The burden of these accounts is that when the elders (parents) are wrong or misguided, they need not be obeyed.

Jesus also talked in very unsentimental ways about a person's obligation to parents, particularly in reference to divided loyalty between discipleship and family. The man who asked to delay following Jesus until he could fulfill his responsibility to his aged father was told, "Follow me, and leave the dead to bury their own dead."[4]

Jesus states it more explicitly in Matthew 10: "He who loves father or mother more than me is not worthy of me; and he who loves son or daughter more than me is not worthy of me."⁵ Clearly Jesus holds that there are more important values than family loyalty. His position becomes unequivocal when told that his mother and brothers are waiting for him while he is teaching: " 'Who is my mother, and who are my brothers?' And stretching out his hand toward his disciples, he said, 'Here are my mother and my brothers! For whoever does the will of my Father in heaven is my brother, and sister, and mother.' "⁶ The urgency of Jesus' mission took precedence over family loyalty. He clearly preached in the Jewish apocalyptic tradition of his day, which expected that very soon the end of history would occur, radically changing all the structures of society into the kingdom of God. In that kingdom family would mean more than blood relationship.

When in the early church that apocalyptic vision fades, we find the writer of the Epistle to the Ephesians supporting a more traditional view of the commandment and urging this as a basis for the ordered structuring of family life: "Children obey your parents in the Lord, for it is right. 'Honor your father and mother' (this is the first commandment with a promise), 'that it may be well with you and that you may live long on the earth.' "⁷

Assumption 3. The family is part of the created order.

Just as virtually all cultures, from the simplest to the most sophisticated, see the family as a foundation for social order, the ancient Hebrew culture, from which Christianity emerged, placed emphasis on the family. The family was understood as a vital part of the created order. Although we have seen that a variety of family forms existed, the family always functioned as an essential part of the social fabric. The family protected and nurtured the new lives that were born into the world until they were able to participate fully in the social order. In a very important way the family, however formed, provides the matrix for the ongoing creative process of the birth and nurture of new generations.

Scripture portrays family life as realized sometimes in imperfect, painful family relations. The biblical accounts honestly describe betrayal and disloyalty, rivalry and animosity, adultery and cheating, in addition to love, trust, protection, and other positive dimensions of family relations.

The Christian view continued this dual theme, which acknowledged the value of the family while at the same time refusing to absolutize it. Because human beings are quite imperfect, families are imperfect means to an end, rather than ends in themselves.

Anderson's *The Family and Pastoral Care* helps us to understand the way in which three major functions of family life—procreation, stability, and individual worth, all of them involving the generations—provide clues for understanding families theologically as well as socially.[8] It doesn't take a family or even a marriage to conceive a child; it only requires a sexually active male and female. But once conception has taken place a long process of protection and nurture are required. Societies have usually believed that this is provided best within a family structure. Sexuality in the context of an organized responsible relationship is the way in which the human race continues in both biological and social dimensions.

Marriage and parenthood in the Christian tradition offer vital ways of serving God. In a sense parents share in the ongoing process of creation. It is serious business. Through procreation humans create links in the generational chain, which runs from the beginning to the end of human history. The ways in which generations, younger and older, interact then make life, health, and development possible. Thus, the creative process results not simply in the fertilization of the ovum but in the years and decades of nurture and development that follow birth.

Seeing the procreative function of the family in this extended way illuminates how the family operates throughout the life of a person, not simply in the early years. We never completely leave our families. The nurturing of each generation, young, middle, and elderly, has an impact on the quality of life for all of them. As each new generation is added and as each older generation dies, the entire family is reconstituted and changes in order to interdependently deal with the new configuration.

In addition to providing for procreation, the family furthers societal stability. Without some patterns of enduring relationships, society would be chaotic and disconnected, like a cloth with all the threads running the same direction. Living in community requires an act of faith because you have to trust that society will not swallow you up; that it is safe to relate to others. Stability is important theologically. It does not mean that things do not change but that they can be trusted. Our families can be the means by which we learn what faith is all about.

Although family forms differ from culture to culture, for most societies the family serves as the primary social unit, the small, manageable group in which people learn to participate in the larger social order. For the past century or so, our Western society has recognized the power of a variety of institutions (schools and churches, youth organizations like the Scouts, television) that supplement the socializing function of the family.

When children are young, parents have the authority to teach—it is hoped in an enlightened fashion—that social living depends on knowing and respecting the rules that assure individual rights and mutual concern. When children become adults, they develop a kind of peer relationship with parents that exists beside remnants of the earlier structure.

The third function of the family is to nurture a sense of individual worth. Psychologists indicate that people develop a sense of personal worth only if regarded as worthwhile by others who are important to them. Ideally the bonding of child and parents that takes place shortly after birth initiates in the child a deep sense of self-esteem; this is affirmed in giving an infant a name and continues in good parenting throughout life.

Part of human development results in our capacity to balance self against others. As we know, inordinate development of the self produces egotism, which alienates a person from others. However, too much emphasis on the place of others in a person's life produces blind conformity and weakness, because he or she is controlled by perceptions of others' responses. Healthy selfhood, developed in the laboratory of the family, has the capacity to keep these two tendencies in creative tension. Healthy selfhood depends on children learning early in family life that they are separate, distinct individuals bound in the family to caring, supportive others. Learning this contributes to the health of both the family and the individual child.

How impoverished life would be if everyone were the same! The family is the key for preparing people to affirm social diversity while still being able to affirm that every person, no matter how different, is a person of worth. Human rights depend on such an affirmation. Children are not to be clones of their parents or of their siblings. Each person is unique, making the family a variegated combination of selves. This variety becomes the basis for the very important social attitudes of tolerance and the celebration of diversity, which Anderson calls "the sign of God's extravagance."[9] In the church baptism affirms selfhood and personal worth in the sight of God.

As children grow, the circle of their relationships expands to include people outside the family: schoolmates and teachers, dates and mates. This expansion introduces them to the element of pluralism: "Our family's way of looking at things is not the only possible way."

Choices and decisions have to be made in a larger context, but a child lives most fully when he or she participates in the community with a sense of being a uniquely worthwhile self.

Assumptions Growing Out of Our Social Class and Culture

Assumption 4. The level of interdependence in living style is influenced by social class.

Although we in a democratic system find the concept of social class difficult, nevertheless, it is an important way of describing differences in the background of various people. Classification becomes a problem if used to attach value judgments to the categories, rather than as merely descriptive.

The middle class is generally regarded as reasonably well-educated, moderately affluent, and as professional or managerial. This group tends to be less rooted than others in a particular community. Persons in the middle class may make numerous career moves, which may separate them by many miles from their siblings and parents. Two qualities highly valued in this group are independence and self-sufficiency. Middle-class people press toward getting ahead and put emphasis on individual effort. Their interdependence may be much more noticeable in their work than in their family life.

Members of the working class tend to be nonprofessional, less well educated, and less affluent than the middle-class. Because most of them do not make many job-related moves, they tend to live in the same community with other family members, so extended family relationships are possible. These produce a climate of intergenerational helpfulness and support. Interdependence is valued both at work and at home. This description holds for closely knit ethnic groups with a strong sense of family solidarity.

Assumption 5. Each generation should take care of itself.

Whatever our class, Western culture communicates two messages about responsibility. First, it affirms responsibility: members of a family clearly have responsibility for one another. But the second message limits that responsibility in a number of ways. Legally our society, for example, frees parents from economic responsibility for their children once they reach the age of majority. It protects adult children by placing limits on the extent to which they must help their elderly parents. To protect the welfare of the generations in the context of such limits, the public sector, in the form of governmental or institutional care, provides assistance. The limitations mirror the way in which our society values private property, independence, and self-sufficiency. Socially, it is not considered proper for the needs of one generation to deplete the resources of another. Although legal protection against this happening is not rigidly applied, the social values hold that each adult generation should take care of itself as much as possible.

Assumption 6. The changing size of the middle generation compared with other generations affects intergenerational caregiving.

The projected demographics for the 1990s show that the growth of the elderly population will continue. For many decades we will be living with the upswings and downswings produced by the baby-boom that followed World War II. This large group of baby-boomers is now beginning to enter middle age, while the smaller number of young adults reflects the smaller families of the baby-boomers themselves. The actual figures are not crucial for us here. What we do need to see is that the generations are unequal in size and that this disproportion changes the whole picture of intergenerational interdependence as the ratio between givers and receivers fluctuates.

Because the middle-aged are the primary intergenerational caregivers, when they are fewer in number additional strain is put on the family system by the upset in balance between needs and resources. For instance, in a few decades, far fewer people than now will be paying into Social Security at a time when the recipients of benefits will be most numerous. In the private sector, there will be fewer middle-aged children to care for elderly parents and for their young adult children.

Assumption 7. Contemporary social changes significantly diminish intergenerational caregiving.

In this century the shape of the family has changed significantly. While the number of nuclear families (father, mother, and children) has increased, noteworthy has been the declining number of extended familes (parents and children plus grandparents, aunts, uncles, cousins available to each other). The nuclear family is a product of urbanization and geographic and social mobility. The nuclear family, as the term implies, puts emphasis on independence, self-sufficiency, and privacy and de-emphasizes a sense of community. It tends to see responsibility as limited to the nuclear family rather than the more extended community and relies for expanded caregiving on outsiders rather than family members.

Another relevant major social change has been in employment patterns. In agrarian and village cultures work life and home life were intertwined. With industrialization, the father as the wage earner spent the entire day away from home. This meant that the mother had much more responsibility for running the home and raising the children than she had had previously. When the father came home from work, home was now to be his refuge, a place where he could rest until it was time for him to go off to work again. From the mid-twentieth century on, a further change has taken place in many families as the wife and mother has gone to work outside the home also. However, most women find that their home responsibilities are not suspended because they are working outside the home. It is impossible for a woman to do all the household work in addition to holding a job, and a whole new industry has grown to ease the homemaker's burden: frozen meals, cleaning services, labor-saving appliances. However, a major area for which little provision has been made is in the supplying of services of intergenerational caregiving in the family home. Most caregiving services can be purchased only outside the home.

The caregiver in an intergenerational household is almost always the daughter or daughter-in-law. This means that today a tension may exist between the very legitimate values of a woman's working outside the home (contributing to family income, finding self-fulfillment in a career, utilizing talents) and the values underlying the role of the woman as intergenerational caregiver.

Although husbands and fathers also have responsibilities as caregivers, they are sheltered by the general social value that affirms, rightly or wrongly, that the male contribution to the family is made at the workplace rather than in the home. It is clear that the emerging more egalitarian style of family life has not made intergenerational caregiving easier.

Another change of our time is the increased number of divorced adult children living alone or as single parents. (In a way this change is modified by the fact that in the past there were more persons who never married or who were widowed.) This change has two impacts on intergenerational care. First, the divorced child often needs help from the middle-aged parents, particularly in reestablishing a home. Second, when a divorced single person becomes the middle generation, he or she needs to accept increased responsibility for the care of aging parents. Since daughters or daughters-in-law usually provide such care, elderly parents have less likelihood of receiving needed care if their son has divorced or if their daughter is a single parent working to support herself and her family.

One of the most far-reaching recent changes makes possible the purchasing of services of a surrogate family. A surrogate family is a variation of one of the strongest cultural values found in most societies: the special nature of the blood relationship. Most of the assumptions of family relationships have been based on the rights and responsibilities of blood relationship. The use of a surrogate family, therefore, has major familial consequences.

The reasons people resort to surrogate families are varied and complex. In some instances, the high value placed on independence and self-sufficiency has caused people to reason: I do not want to burden my family with my care, so I will purchase the care I need from those who give it well. This reasoning is often found in those entering retirement communities that have life-care facilities. In other instances, personal circumstances or the kinds of social changes we have just described make it impossible to care for a young adult child or an aged parent. Finally, distance and the breakdown of family structure have loosened personal ties, and the sense of responsibility has been loosened as well.

Assumption 8. The public sector is increasingly involved in meeting generational needs.

Until a few decades ago, in our society there were public institutions for meeting situations of extreme need: orphanages, alms houses, and poor farms. Because these dealt with only a few unfortunate people, those who received such care were often stigmatized.

Two major changes took place in the last half century. Not only were the programs of government benefits broadened to cover many more situations of need and potential need, but these benefits were made available to nearly everyone in the society. We see rather clearly that the more people who are eligible for a benefit, the less social stigma it carries. When everyone qualifies, such benefits are construed as rights. Outstanding examples are Social Security and Medicare, which have become financial resources for the majority of elderly persons in our society, thus easing the responsibility of their adult children. While it might be argued that their children pay into the system through the Social Security tax, it is still true that elderly parents receiving the benefit are helped by many people who are also contributing.

Many communities subsidize housing facilities for elderly persons with low incomes. In most communities a broad spectrum of services are available through federal and state Offices of Aging. Many of these focus on helping the elderly to maintain self-sufficient, independent living for as long as possible.

Other welfare programs are part of the public sector support of needs calling for intergenerational help, such as public assistance and Aid to Dependent Children. To these we could add the supplemental income and Medicaid programs for Social Security beneficiaries in special need. Because a person has to demonstrate a special level of need to qualify for these programs, the programs often carry a stigma, which may dilute their helpfulness.

Another form of public sector support has come through government enforcement of child support requirements after a divorce. While there may be occasional inequities, generally the laws of the states recognize that the responsibilities of parenthood do not terminate with divorce. Child support can ease the cost of intergenerational care that divorced families with children require.

We should note that one of the greatest needs of single parents and working parents is for competent child care. At present, public sector participation in such child care, other than the public schools, is largely limited to the welfare classification. In spite of a desperately growing need for child care, it is not perceived to have the universality that would make it a right, like Social Security or public education.

Assumption 9. The private sector increasingly participates in meeting generational needs.

The growth of pension funds has provided a measure of economic security for the later years of life that has helped relieve some of the needs of the elderly. Another very important private sector development has been the cluster of residential facilities for the elderly: retirement communities, life-care units, and nursing homes. These meet many of the housing and physical-care needs of elderly parents, provided, of course, that the elderly can afford them. Much the same could be said for the development of private, profit-making day-care facilities, which provide services for small children of working parents.

Dealing with Change

The numerous changes just mentioned are not trivial; they have effectively created massive problems with regard to intergenerational relationships. We could merely lament change and long for the good old days "when people believed in family values." It is probably a much more creative option to recognize that history demonstrates that adaptability to change is essential to survival. If we have faith in the creative process that is taking place, the "on-goingness" of creation, we can meaningfully participate in such adaptation. Historically, we *will* participate—whether we want to or not! We can, however, intentionally try to adapt to changing circumstances and infinite variety. By doing so, we have an opportunity to bring forth something new, positive, and enduring.

Anderson writes: "The Creator must 'constantly make new' in order to counter our efforts to diminish God's creative work by limiting change."[10] The ways in which families respond to the changes required by the kinds of intergenerational needs and tensions we are describing can be seen as possibilities for new creations in family life and in the lives of the persons involved.

Assumption 10. Interdependence is the most helpful way to organize intergenerational caregiving.

Another major assumption asserts the central role that must be played by interdependence. We have to resist the notion that the only options are dependence and independence. So much of the mythology of individualism that guides our lives promotes rugged independence and looks down upon dependence as weakness.

Interdependence as a necessary feature of life is supported by modern developmental psychology. Although we must be concerned for the development of individuals, we clearly recognize that this happens in relationship; a self in isolation is not a healthy, well-developed self. As mentioned earlier, positive self development begins with early family relationships in which a very young person is helped to feel wanted, cared for, and loved by others in the family. An infant is totally dependent, because he or she cannot do anything to meet the physical and emotional needs that are crucial to survival. As the child grows, he or she experiences increasing independence and decreasing dependence. This process occurs, hopefully, in a context of increasing interdependence, in which the self and the family both give and receive, enhancing everyone in the process. At the far end of the aging process, it is possible but not inevitable that the balance shifts radically from interdependence back to dependence. The aged person's resources may be so depleted that giving seems an impossibility. However, memory of that person's past contribution may keep the web of interdependence intact.

Developmental psychology has focused on the process by which a self is differentiated from family through the process of developing a personal identity. It is so easy to construe that process simply as a movement toward independence. If that were true, humans would be like some lower animal forms in which the young separate from their mothers as soon as weaned, and no relationship continues. In contrast, human beings do differentiate slowly, but in the context of interdependence. Moving through developmental tasks in succession, as a person moves from one generation to another, supports the concept of interdependence. We have a sense of "I did that task when I was your age; now it's your turn" or "You did that task for me; now I do it for you."

Assumption 11. Every generation has the possibility for growth.

Developmental psychology assures us that every stage of life, from the youngest to the oldest, has its growing edge. When dealing with any generation, one of the important questions to ask is "What possibilities for growth exist here?" Especially vital in those situations that are increasingly constricting and limiting, this question seeks for growth possibilities as a way of breaking the tyranny of limitations. Often with the best of intentions, we make people overly dependent by not being aware of their possibilities for growth, no matter how small these might be. An interdependent pattern of relationship makes such awareness easier, and such awareness increases interdependence, as others' growth can often inform our own.

Another way to think of this is to affirm that each generation has a right to fulfillment in its own way. One can be fulfilled as a child, as a middle-aged person, or as an elderly adult. These fulfillments may be quite different, but nevertheless real. We risk doing violence to people if we assume that personal fulfillment is not possible for them or if the personal fulfillment we envision for them is unrealistically inappropriate to their generation.

Assumption 12. We live as a covenant people.

Anderson aptly describes covenant within families:

> The interdependence that is inherent in all creation is finally sustained by humankind through intentional commitment or covenant. . . . Covenant, even more than commitment, is an apt metaphor for understanding interdependence within the family because it assumes a relationship of mutuality.[11]

In the ancient covenants with Israel, God says not only "I am committed to you" but also "You are committed to me." The intergenerational care we have discussed so far does not propose one generation caring for another but two or more generations committed to caring for each other.

The quality of an interdependent relationship, however, can range from a crude barter arrangement ("You've got what I need, and I've got what you need. Let's trade!") to an enlightened mutuality ("Through our need for each other, we both can grow to be fuller persons."). By expressing interdependence as covenant, we lift it from the simple level of tit-for-tat and excessive self-interest. A covenant is based on trust, trust that we are loved and cared for even when we are not able to return as much as we receive. Scripture bases covenant on the relationship between God and persons or nations. In that relationship it is not generally assumed that humans provide more than they receive or that the relationship is one of equivalence. Covenantal relationship does assume the biblical understanding of mutual love, a genuine desire on the part of each to enhance the other, a trust that one person will not be exploited in the relationship, and confidence in the possibility of new life.

Some folks who cherish illusions of their self-sufficiency find interdependence threatening, because it necessarily acknowledges that their future is not entirely in their own hands. Their future is also in part controlled by the needs of others. This is why the middle aged feel caught in the middle. With their future very much affected by their children's needs (regardless of their ages) and the needs of their elderly parents, it is at the same time shaped by what their children and their parents continue to give to them.

Taking a covenant seriously very often reveals us to ourselves. We recognize that we sometimes lack faithfulness to the covenant; we do not do our share. Anyone who has experienced the parent-child covenant knows the feelings of guilt that come when he or she sees missed opportunities, mishandled crises, discipline that misfired. Being aware of living in a serious covenant relationship makes us see our failures, and we experience guilt. But being in a covenant relationship also offers us a remedy for that guilt, because, in the theological sense, covenant implies grace. In the ancient covenant with Israel, God never stopped loving the people, even when they failed dramatically in their part of the relationship. John Calvin's phrase has become a theological truism: grace precedes repentance. This crystalizes a remarkable insight. Before we even think about repenting, we know that forgiveness is given. In fact, only because we know that we will be forgiven can we muster the courage to repent.

In a covenant relationship between the generations, we do not earn what we receive; we find it given to us because of our interdependence. In spite of the fact that no one, no generation, gives or receives perfectly, the wonderful possibility is held out to us that the interdependent process itself, the reminder that our lives are woven inextricably together, brings each person closer to fulfillment of selfhood and relation to God.

Chapter 3

A Values Crunch with the Younger Generation

The tensions that often develop between middle-aged parents and their young adult children arise from a collision between the values of these two generations. Conflict is a natural outgrowth of the process that begins in earnest when children are adolescents and continues into young adulthood.

The entry into mid-life is not sharply delineated. We cannot say, for example, "Today is your forty-fifth birthday—welcome to middle age!" Most parents have the experience of dealing with adolescent children shortly before they begin to regard themselves as middle aged.

The crisis that then develops with adolescent children often stimulates the first parental realization that they have moved over onto the older side of the generation gap. Aware that society expects them to shape and guide their children, parents disturbingly see their guidance met with questioning and resistance on the part of their children. Simultaneously parents' anxieties increase as they question the ability of their children to cope with the growing complexities of society and their lives.

Generations as Communicators of Values

By the time a child reaches adolescence, most parents have not been the child's primary instructors for many years. The growing child has spent more hours each day with school teachers, peers, and television than with parents and has been considerably influenced by these surrogates.

The communication of values between generations flows two ways. The older generation seeks to transmit its values to the younger, passing on the standards to which they have been committed personally. As the younger generation tests those values, it can often contribute different insights and reshape the family values in new ways.

Each generation, based on its own experience, perceives life somewhat differently. We naively assume that the values adopted by persons in one generation will perfectly fit another generation. To communicate values intergenerationally, then, is both necessary and frustrating.

Often for the first time, parents of adolescents experience a sense of powerlessness. The disciplinary measures they had used to control the pliant young child no longer work. Adolescents can comply with their parents' values at home, but parents cannot be sure by what standards the adolescent lives during the many hours spent in other settings.

Both adolescents and parents approaching middle age confront emerging value issues with ambivalence. The adolescent yearns for independence from home and the world of his or her parents and at the same time feels apprehensive about giving up the security of the dependent relationship. While the parents want the child to become more and more independent and increasingly his or her own person, at the same time they are fearful that the adolescent may be ill-prepared for independence.

This ambivalence in both generations produces a great deal of inconsistency and fluctuation between the values of dependence and independence, control and freedom. Poor communication may cause the behavior of parents and child to be misunderstood by each other. Confusing signals are given, and reception is blurry. Overreactions occur, stirred by anxieties; positions polarize; acts of repression or defiance escalate.

An impasse can be broken only when the actors in the family drama realize that interdependence offers the most productive mode for relationships. Through a process of communication, which takes into account the ambivalence everyone feels, the parties can realize that *each* generation has need of the other and that *each* generation has a contribution to make to the process of ongoing personal and interpersonal development. In a sense, a new contract for parenting can emerge from such a communication process. The generation gap continues to exist, but it can be bridged.

Issues of Authority and Power

Many of us will know the struggle of the adolescent for power twice in our lives, first as adolescents and then as adults dealing with adolescents. This change of perspective can make adolescence seem a very new experience, not something the adult has ever experienced before.

All societies provide boundaries for inter-generational conflict. Other cultures mistakenly regarded as "primitive" by our standards have developed initiation rites for a gradual transfer of authority. These rites channel in socially approved ways the biological and social impulses that emerge in adolescence and assure that some power is given to young people as they begin to take their place in young adult society. Such clearly patterned ritual responses recognize that to release too much authority too soon disrupts the social balance and puts too much responsibility on the inexperienced younger generation.

Our "more sophisticated" American culture is notably deficient in initiation rites. Few effective channels exist to allow young people to make a positive response to their growing demand for authority and power. Although our adolescents, like those in other cultures, experience biological changes and emerging impulses to take a more active role in society, our culture, instead of providing ways for responding positively to these impulses, sends the message "Wait!"

Adolescents react by forming their own youth subculture, in which very often they dramatize their sense of alienation by acting out disdain for adult standards and values. Punk rock provides a classic illustration in our time. This phenomenon, with its exotic hair styles and bizarre costumes, expresses a kind of symbolic revenge on the part of youth feeling excluding by being told to wait for power. Dramatically they state to the adult world: "You won't give us the authority to make our own decisions, so we'll make them in our own way and show you that we don't care, because we don't want your old life-style anyway." Youth have been put in the position of demanding power in an exaggerated confrontation we call the generation gap.

Issues of Trust

Intergenerational struggles around power and authority often center on issues of trust. Between childhood and adolescence the risk factor escalates. Young people spend more and more time away from home with the peer group; a driver's license is their passport to freedom; drugs and alcohol are readily available to them; and the possibility that they can become sexually active increases. Parents agonize over the questions "Can I trust my child to avoid disaster?" "Can I trust my child to live in accordance with the values the family has taught?" The adolescent, on the other hand, interprets the parents' caution and responds by saying something like the following: "You don't trust me!" or "You can trust me!" or "You should trust me!"

Once the parents recognize that the adolescent must be given increasing freedom to enable growth into adulthood, becoming trustful is the only alternative to experiencing agonizing anxiety. But we all know that issues of freedom stir up a storm in many families. Eva Leveton describes what she calls the "trust trap," which makes the mistake of confusing parental trust with parental love.[1] Love is something that is (or should be) inherent in the parent-child relationship. In most families it is assured; no matter what the child is or does, the love continues. Trust, however, is not a given; it is *earned* by a person's building a record of reasonably living up to responsibilities. Trustworthiness builds gradually as a young person learns to be faithful to responsibility and demonstrates that he or she is guided by values that the parents can support. If the adolescent fails to accept responsibility adequately, his or her trustworthiness diminishes for a time and must be reestablished.

Balanced Attitudes Toward Freedom and Authority

The need to balance freedom and authority produces a learning experience for both parents and children. Children gradually learn that they have to assume a sense of responsibility for themselves and that actions have consequences that must be accepted. Parents must be concerned to regulate the increments of increased freedom so that the consequences of the decisions of the young person are manageable, even though they may be difficult. Parents fear most the disastrous consequences from wrong decisions, the irreversible damage to their child or to others.

This anxiety causes some parents to restrict their children's freedom too much. Overrestraint tends to produce one of two consequences. A rebellious young person fights against it, ignores it, or violates the restraint; alternately, a young person anxious not to be rejected by parents becomes very rigid in moral judgments, slavishly obedient to external authority, and unable to make his or her own responsible decisions. Both of these response patterns have implications for young adulthood.

John J. Mitchell proposes that we make a grave error by focusing too much on early adolescence and the struggle to leave childhood and not enough on later adolescence and the struggle of the emerging adult.[2] Mitchell objects to our dealing with adolescents as grown-up children rather than as young adults. By doing so, he states, we constantly draw a line of restraint for the adolescent to demonstrate that he or she is more child than adult. This prepares negatively for the developmental stage toward which the adolescent is moving. Mitchell argues that we demean adolescents by treating them as large, contentious children; a more constructive approach acknowledges that late adolescents have needs more like those of adults than of children.

Mitchell writes:

> Adolescence is largely wasted because our society refuses to let the adolescent grow, contribute, and define himself in terms of creative addition. . . . The adolescent predicament . . . is a disorder which comes about when a person who considers himself important is expected to *comply* without having the right to *contribute*.[3]

Adolescents have a need for involvement, a need to contribute to their family, a need to be regarded as important. Although we may begin communicating values to adolescents when they are growing out of childhood, we need to make a transition to communicating values to young people who are entering the adult world. This means that parents cannot expect unthinking obedience to parental authority, but that they need to anticipate the need to support rationally the acceptance of values they want to pass on to their adolescents. This begins a process of enabling adolescents to make rational judgments about the values that will guide them.

Values: Religious and Moral

The work of Lawrence Kohlberg[4] has helped us to see that moral development, the way in which one responds to values, changes with personal maturity and integration. While not an automatic process linked to chronological age, there is a possible progression through six stages of moral development, according to Kohlberg's model.

Kohlberg calls the first two stages "preconventional." In the first stage one does what is right based on the fear of punishment. In the second stage doing what is right is oriented toward procuring something in return. Both of these stages focus attention on what the person receives from a particular behavior, either in punishment or reward. Moral decisions are based heavily on others' response, with little or no thought given to the "rightness" of the behavior itself.

The next two stages are "conventional," a somewhat more sophisticated refinement of the first two. In the third stage a person is concerned for the approval of others, for not disrupting relationships. He or she conforms to the values of others in order to be well thought of. In the fourth stage the person is extremely conscious of the rules. Following the rules constitutes good behavior. In this stage, sometimes called the law-and-order stage, the person feels a good deal of guilt when he or she breaks the norms.

Kohlberg calls the final two stages "postconventional." In the fifth stage the person finally breaks out of being controlled by others and by their reactions and develops the ability to regulate his or her own behavior. The person recognizes that unless people exercise a measure of self-control, social existence becomes very difficult. People can get along because a social contract protects their individual rights and keeps them from taking undue advantage of one another.

The sixth stage refers to the development of a healthy conscience. An individual does the right thing because he or she believes it to be right, rather than because of what others will think or do. The person's conduct is integrated; his or her selfhood rings true.

Kohlberg suggests that a great many adults still function at stages three or four, while some achieve the fifth stage. If his assessment is accurate, we should not be surprised at the fact that many adolescents and young adults experience a certain confusion in the lessons they learn from parents and mentors.

Questions of Meaning

The answers to the question "What has meaning?" create crucial reference points for anyone trying to navigate a course through life. The more stormy, stressful periods of life make these reckoning points all the more necessary.

According to developmental understanding, the two periods in which we ask this question of meaning most pointedly are adolescence and middle age. To work out an emergent identity and begin to assume dimensions of adulthood, an adolescent must learn to distinguish what really counts in life. The values that have been communicated by family, school, peers, and heroes are examined. Adolescents adopt some, modify others, and reject still others. We shall see shortly some of the kinds of issues that the young adult grapples with in this values-testing process.

In middle age a person tends to have another go at this process, which composes a part of the so-called mid-life crisis. Having settled into a more or less routine life of work and responsibility and having achieved or modified most of the goals that previously opened up new possibilities, the person in mid-life reaches a plateau. This provokes a time of reappraisal. Many middle-aged persons ask, "What has meaning for me now?" They are looking for the reference points that will guide them for the rest of life's course. Some middle-aged parents find that they now question the very values they had presented with reasonable certainty to their adolescent and young adult children only a few years earlier.

This change makes possible a new level of generational interdependence. Sometimes the input the late adolescent and young adult children made during that extended dialogue was taken seriously by the parents and incorporated into their lives. For example, the younger generation likely strongly supported the value of being free to "be your own self," "do your own thing." They stressed independence and insisted on not being overwhelmed by responsibility for the future, on "living for the moment." They saw the possibility of meaningful relationships without everlasting commitments. Some middle-aged parents who appraised these values upon entering their own period of reassessment may have heeded their children's instruction and modified their own views. People gave up relatively secure jobs to start "second careers." Middle-aged parents, as cited in Eda LeShan in the previous chapter, decided that they did not have to sacrifice their own interests because of responsibilities toward the younger or older generations. If they wanted to travel or enter some new ventures, they could use their financial resources rather than simply conserving them for others to inherit. The high incidence of middle-age divorce may well reflect the values of the younger generation: that relationships, even meaningful relationships, do not necessarily go on forever.

The values that help us to determine the meaning of life shift with time, at least in the living of them. Of course, loving is always superior to hating; helping is more to be desired than hurting. These seem to be enduring and true values. But the ways in which we love or help may change from generation to generation; or what one generation may see as helping, another may perceive as hurting.

Christians have always been challenged, and sometimes troubled, by the New Testament teaching that we are *"in* but *not of* the world." Some Christians draw the line between the church and the world very clearly; for others the division is more difficult to find. Most of us can remember when many church people defined the "world" as dancing, playing cards, and going to movies and were adamant in their opposition to such "worldliness." At the same time these people found nothing wrong with racially segregated churches or hateful sectarianism. So we have to be careful and circumspect when we differentiate our Christian family values from the values of the world.

It is helpful in the communication of values to offer an interpretation of the rationale behind the affirmation of particular values. This is particularly true in light of Mitchell's proposal to regard adolescents as emergent adults rather than as grown-up children. When we communicate values to younger children, we often do so solely on the basis of parental authority: "You are expected to behave according to these values because these are the values our family affirms without question." In contrast, both Mitchell and Kohlberg argue that more mature moral development takes place when values are communicated in adult fashion, rationally and objectively. Persons then can commit themselves to accepting a particular value, not simply because someone else affirms it, but because they understand and accept the opportunities and responsibilities that grow out of acknowledging that value. The ways in which people worked out these values during the time of adolescence will have a major bearing on the quality of the relationship between middle-aged parents and their young adult children.

Leaving Home

Most young adult children of middle-aged parents have established themselves on their own turf. They went away to college, to work, to military service; came home intermittently; and finally established their own homes. In many families this was preceded by the child's gradually leaving home emotionally, that is, being less dependent on parents for guidance and influence and more dependent on peer relationships. The way in which this leaving home was handled both physically and emotionally by the parents has an important influence on the quality of ongoing relationships with young adult children.

We often refer to this time in the lives of middle-aged parents as the "empty nest" period. Anderson reminds us that "the image of the 'empty nest' is much too negative. . . . It implies that families are only for children. The family of origin is re-forming itself during this epoch when new family units are being formed."[5] Not only is this a time when the middle-aged parents reshape their relationship to each other; they also now form a new mode of relating to their young adult children.

The physical separation of the generations involves the potential for both pain and celebration. An important step in development, it also symbolizes the ending of an era. Old loyalties shift; old patterns of authority change; old dependencies end. The ambivalent feelings aroused by such a separation affect both the young adult child and the middle-aged parents.

As long as parents are living, a son or daughter can always relate to his or her original home. As Anderson puts it: "It is important for both children and parents to understand that we leave home so that we can go home again. How children leave—and how parents let them go—will affect how easy it will be to return."[6]

We are very much accustomed to thinking of loving as holding, hugging, embracing. Loving is also letting go, allowing a person to develop into a unique self. In our Christian heritage we see this two-dimensional fullness of love in the theological concept of grace. We experience both aspects of love in the grace-filled love of God: in the words of the hymn "O Love, That Will Not Let Me Go" and in the love of the father for the prodigal son, which grants freedom, even freedom to make serious mistakes. This love, interpreted theologically as a paradox or tension, is mirrored in the situation of the middle-aged parent letting children go.

That paradoxical quality of love costs something. There is real pain in giving someone the freedom to grow. Eda LeShan suggests that the cost of giving maturing children freedom to grow is balanced by the reward of middle-aged parents in finding an opportunity for their own growing in a new freedom from responsibility.[7]

This new way of loving, both the love of the adult child and the love of the middle-aged parent, produces an adaptation of the family system. Love requires new styles of relating as peers, and new patterns of belonging. As long as we live, we are our children's parents, but we relate with a new form of interdependence that testifies to the growing maturity of both parent and child. Leaving and letting go does not have to mean the end of loving; in fact, it can be an important way of giving love.

Drugs and Alcohol

Unless the two generations are separated by many miles and have little contact, middle-aged parents remain concerned, as they were during adolescence, with the life-style of the younger generation. An emotionally charged arena for this tension in values involves drug or alcohol use and abuse. Most parents are understandably anxious about the availability of alcohol and drugs to adolescents and their continued use by young adults. Unhappily, in many families use of alcohol and drugs become part of the acting-out process of adolescent rebellion, when adolescents try to claim adult status by emulating what they perceive to be young adult or adult behavior. Such use continues to be part of the young adult's experience either as a habit or as a compulsive way of trying to cope with life.

Parents hope that their own values will prevent their children from becoming involved in substance abuse. Contemporary experience indicates that often parents do not successfully influence their children's substance use. Young people from reasonably solid families experiment with substances or become habitual users, much to the pain of their parents.

Does this mean that the values of the parents were deficient, that they were not able to communicate them adequately, that the family influence was ineffective? Perhaps, but there is the distinct possibility that the onslaught of changes in cultural values was so great that only some families were able to assert their own values. Some parents experience this onslaught as an increased sense of inadequacy and powerlessness. Parents' own use of alcohol and drugs also obviously affects their children's actions. Much still needs to be learned about alcohol and drug abuse, but the growth of research, awareness, and support groups (such as Adult Children of Alcoholics) have provided healing and insight for many families.

Career Choices

There once was a time when the choice of a person's future occupation was totally determined by the family. Either the child continued in the family occupation or profession, or the family pressed its ambitions for upward occupational mobility onto him or her. This period of time was followed by a time when many families very intentionally let their hands off career choices: "You make your own decision!"

Lightly hidden under the family's posture is a value-orientation. Some families or some young adults will candidly admit that they support a career choice that will lead to financial security. Other families or young people will opt for a service motivation even though this limits income. The degree to which altruism is a value communicated by the family will have bearing on a person's career choice. In terms of intergenerational tensions, stresses occur only when there is a significant difference of viewpoint and values between parents and young adult children. If there is a consensus on values, whatever they be, there will be little tension.

Sexual Ethics

Along with alcohol and drug abuse, sexuality presents the most sensitive issue involving parents and young adult children. Sexual relationship may be so crucial because it always involves not a single person but at least two. The issue is further complicated by the fact that sexual activity is based on a natural and inevitable biological development. We would have serious concern with the adolescent or young adult who did not experience sexual stirrings. At the same time our society reveals anxiety about the control of these natural impulses by erecting barriers against their expression.

Moral confusion is a natural consequence of this tension between biological growth and social expectations. Most families have been well aware of sexuality as an issue since their children were adolescents. Parents may feel that they did not do a particularly good job at addressing the values that shape sexual behavior. The arena of sexuality defines the place where many young people have left family life, narrowly understood, and moved into a wider social existence, often with limited involvement of their parents.

Certainly in most communities peer pressure supports a young person's becoming sexually active. Most parents have strong anxiety about sexually active children and have tried to teach values that would prohibit such behavior. We have to acknowledge that in many instances such moral instruction has not been terribly effective. In our time there is increased moral tolerance for sexually active adolescents.

Furstenburg reports:

There are several reasons why the influence of parents is so slight. First, it appears that most parents do not want to get directly involved and, certainly, most teenagers are reluctant to encourage involvement. Most parents would prefer that their teens defer sexual activity, but seem resigned to the fact that their views are not likely to be the single determining factor.[8]

Similarly, it is pointed out that there exists a much higher incidence of sexual activity of adolescents who feel unhappy and cut off at home, where communication with parents is strained.[9]

To Marry or Not to Marry

The point at which the values crunch over sexuality surfaces very commonly for middle-aged parents of young adult children is over the question of their marrying or living with another person. A generation ago it was completely unacceptable for a man and a woman to live together without being married. We called it "living in sin," either seriously or facetiously. Now, a good many families have had to accommodate to a son or daughter living with a significant other without the commitment of marriage. The very fact that we do not have a suitable word in the English language for the person who is living with our adult child indicates both the newness of the phenomenon and our ambivalence toward it.

Many of the people who live in such relationships acknowledge that theirs are loving relationships, that they want something more than a casual relationship, that they take marriage so seriously they do not feel ready to make the enduring commitments marriage asks. They reject both promiscuity and irresponsibility in their sexual relationships. A few are acting out disdain for marriage, which they have come to regard as a hollow institution that rarely approximates its ideal form. Many others are open to the possibility of marriage in the future. In particular, if they decide to have a child, they would feel ready to make the commitment involved in being married.

Parents who are called upon to accept an unmarried relationship in the adult child's life often do not do so easily. They are concerned for social stigma, for the implication that they have somehow failed in the moral education of their child. Parents who gradually accommodate themselves to the situation, do so usually on an intellectual level at first, because they love their child and do not want to be alienated from him or her by forcing the child to choose between the significant other and themselves. They also recognize that the child's decision to "live together" is not a total violation of the moral values they taught but often is based on these very same values: the importance of love, the seriousness of the marital commitments, and the desirability of being reasonably sure that the selection of a mate is one that will lead to a happy and positive relationship.

The initial intellectual acceptance comes after a process of rationalization, in the best sense of the word, over a period of time. The emotional testing of the accommodation usually comes when the couple visit the parental home. We have conventions for relating to a son-in-law or daughter-in-law but no similar conventions for relating to a live-in partner. In marriage there is social recognition that one becomes a member of the spouse's family, but what of a less permanent, less committed relationship?

The acid emotional test in many families occurs if the couple visit overnight in the family home. What will be the sleeping arrangements? The values that have been taught in the past, no sex outside of marriage, would require that they occupy separate rooms. Even though everyone acknowledges that they have been living intimately in their own space, such intimacy in the family home has a special impact. For the family to permit or not to permit the couple's occupying the same bed under the family roof communicates important value statements. A negative decision may reflect an effort to uphold the values that reject all sexual relationship outside marriage. A positive decision can be an affirmation that family love for the adult child and regard for the partner is of higher value than conventional sexual norms. Once that affirmation has been made, people may feel liberated for new possibilities, and a kind of normalcy can return to the family system.

Where Is the Church in This?

Because this study of intergenerational tensions in middle age is being made in the context of families related to the church, it is highly appropriate to ask the question "What is the role of the church in all of this?" One way to answer that question is to look at the kinds of concerns that can guide the church's pastoral caring for middle-aged parents and their adolescent and young adult children.

Pastoral caring here refers to all dimensions of the church's life that seek to care for, nurture, guide, and support persons and their families as they struggle to communicate values between the generations. The church's stake in the values crunch between generations is high, because the church has traditionally been a major guardian and teacher of values in society. The massive shifts in values we have been discussing call for a response from the church, a response that will shape its pastoral caring.

Some people in the church would stiffen their position to defend families against the changes that are taking place. They see values as eternal verities, which cannot be changed or reinterpreted but must be rigidly affirmed. This view often puts the church more and more out of touch with its people. A striking example in our time is the continued resistance by the hierarchy of the Roman Catholic Church to birth-control methods (other than the rhythm method or abstinence) and the wide-spread adoption of the condemned techniques by the majority of Roman Catholics in the industrialized West. If the church will not change its position, it must recognize the defiance of its official teaching by many of its members. There are similar issues within the Protestant churches.

A second kind of response to shifting values is abdication of moral leadership by the church. When some Christians see adherence to their formerly unquestioned values eroded and their efforts to teach them as futile, they act out their disappointment through silent, benign neglect. Their disappointment is rarely put into words because it is too painful.

A third response for the church is to continue functioning as a moral teacher with a flexible approach. Change requires constant reassessment of values, which involves not an abandonment of values but a reinterpretation and prioritizing of those norms. Reassessment is not the same as surrender or compromise with the latest fad. As the hymn writer sings, "New occasions teach new duties."[10]

We have seen how middle-aged parents often need to balance love for their child with affirmation of certain values. This process is sometimes complex and agonizing. Their church needs to stand with them rather than against them in this struggle. Only if the church can be flexible in its support of a complex value system can it respond with pastoral sensitivity.

A very basic focus for pastoral caring (usually provided either in the educational program of the church or through pastoral counseling) is to assist people to understand and implement the ways individuals are simultaneously set apart and joined. As we have stressed earlier, this is a crucial learning from the moment we are separated from our mother's body at birth. A delicate balance between concerns for the self and for other people must be fine-tuned every day of our lives. After the infant leaves the mother's body, it depends totally on mothering and fathering for many months for its survival. Independence at this stage of live would mean death. Only as the child grows does some independence gradually replace total dependence. Once an adolescent has achieved a reasonable sense of identity, the tension between dependence and independence can be balanced in interdependence.

Because the church embodies concern for how people relate to each other, it can be sensitive to the needs of every person in a family system. The very young and very old need to be sheltered from domination, even though their situation inevitably makes them dependent. Those who are developing and maturing at every stage between early childhood and old age can benefit from guidance in the acceptance of responsibility according to their ability to exercise it.

Yet another function of the church speaks to the self-evaluation that is a natural part of middle age. As middle-aged persons begin to reflect on the fact that their lives are half over, they begin to take stock of their accomplishments and failures and reassess their goals in life. For the first time, the limits of life force themselves into the picture, and people face the spiritual crisis of finding the meaning of their lives.

This crisis is dramatically presented, as we have seen, in the tensions that develop between parents and their adolescent and young adult children. As divergent values between the generations and the consequences of these values become apparent, a great deal of responsibility for failure is accepted by contemporary parents. Eda LeShan writes:

> We are the first generation to blame ourselves for everything that ever went wrong with our children. We are the generation that were told we were responsible for the mental health—or lack of it—in our children. . . . Our parents—and all parents before them—assumed that if a child turned out peculiarly, it was a freak of nature, somewhere along the line he must have inherited some "bad blood" from an in-law! . . . Our ancestors were never burdened with the horrible idea that their attitudes, their childraising procedures, were in any way responsible for how their children turned out.[11]

The truth is probably somewhere between total responsibility with its abject guilt and no responsibility. Of course, a number of factors contribute to the successes and failures in our children's lives. Parents certainly have some responsibility, but there are inborn dispositions that help to shape a person, as well as the potent influence of society as a whole, including schools and peers.

Dealing with guilt then becomes a pastoral issue. It involves proper assessment of the guilt that is warranted, acceptance of appropriate responsibility, forgiveness, and making amends. Pastoral caring conveys grace, a healing love that we experience in spite of not having earned it. Middle age, no less than the rest of life, requires grace. Increasingly aware of limitation, of not being able to make everything work, of having important areas of life beyond our control, of failing to exercise many responsibilities wisely and well, perhaps we can arrive at a point of saying, "I tried. I did the best I could." These words do not make an excuse. Rather they acknowledge that our efforts, even our best efforts, very often do not suffice by themselves. We have to depend on Providence, and upon many other resources not our own, in order to hope that things will work out well.

The other side of this issue is that we sometimes actually do fail. We make serious mistakes; we allow our own self-centeredness to interfere; we mishandle others. Our Christian faith says that it is possible to admit our mistakes, our wrong attitudes and actions. We can be forgiven such errors and can be moved to try to turn things around in a positive direction. The pastoral caring of the church can help that to happen.

Chapter 4

The Empty Nest Revisited

Several recent studies indicate that an increasing number of adult children continue to live in or return to live in the home of their parents. Some are unemployed or underemployed and cannot afford to live away from home. Some find it necessary to live at home while they complete college. For economic reasons, as well as a general social trend, the age for getting married has risen. This postpones the time when young adults establish their own homes. Unmarried mothers who choose to keep their babies often live in the family home. When the marriage of an adult child dissolves, resulting either in separation or divorce, the child may see as attractive the option—if it exists—of returning to live with the parents.

Although some families experience serious problems as a result of the empty-nest syndrome, most of them would agree, as a number of studies indicate, that the emptying of the nest has a positive effect on the parents' relationship. Social scientists often describe the series of events leading to the completion of the parents' task of child rearing as the "launching of children," just as shipbuilders launch their completed construction. The term indicates that the entire building process has focused on enabling the children to have a new beginning, a voyage away from the place of origin.

A number of advantages occur in most homes when children have left. "One explanation of greater marital quality following the launching of children may be the generally high level of psychological well-being that has been found to accompany the completion of child-rearing."[1] Couples can spend more time with each other and relax in greater privacy, troubled by fewer occasions for intergenerational tensions. They can use money for their own objectives that formerly went to support their children. And the division of labor that the complex responsibilities of child-raising produced may no longer be required, enabling couples to share work at home. While it is not quite "paradise regained" for most parents, the empty nest does offer them opportunity for beginning a new era of their lives together.

This process can be impeded or reversed if the nest is revisited. Jill Suitor points out that in a study of 677 elderly people in the Boston area,

> contrary to the expectations, the analysis indicated that the presence of adult children had no effect on elderly parents' marital conflict, even when age, educational attainment and gender were controlled. An analysis of the data on respondents sharing a residence with an adult child showed that marital conflict was strongly related to frequent parent-child conflict.[2]

In other words, after the launching of the children, intergenerational tensions can disrupt the relational gains made by parents if children come back home to live.

The Empty Nest Revisited = Dependency Revisited

Thomas Wolfe's title *You Can't Go Home Again* is only partially true. It is true that "home" is always changing with the passage of time, so a person never goes back to exactly the same place. But even so, for the vast majority there is something enduring about home. While parents are living, home continues to exist. However, the return to the nest can occur in several ways: physical, emotional, or financial.

Returning home can be physical. Although an adult child may have established his or her own home, the ending of a marriage may make it impossible to maintain that home. Returning to the parental roof may provide the alternative. However, Wolfe's title expresses something meaningful. Home is still there, but the people involved are different, now reconstituting the family as an adult intergenerational household.

The return "home" can be emotional rather than physical. A hurting adult child may turn to middle-aged parents for primary emotional support, even while living under a separate roof. The adult child is feeling very vulnerable and, as in childhood, turns to parents for major comfort and support. This is a return to the lap rather than a return to the family house.

Or the return to parents may be financial, reflecting a time of monetary need. Whereas adulthood had brought financial independence for a while, changing circumstances returned the child to the parents for a support structure that had operated for many years in earlier life.

Regardless of which of these three modes best describes the empty nest revisited, all involve a return to a pattern of dependency that an adult child had left. Often this is viewed as a retreat for the adult child and a renewed burden for the middle-aged parents.

If the return to dependency becomes protracted or if the arrangement solidifies into the parent-child roles of former years, the phenomenon is called re-parenting. The family faces a complex decision: whether or not to return in this way to a family structure that had been replaced by a peer relationship between adult child and adult parent.

Because our culture prizes independence over dependence, when people are faced with the possible return to dependency, they may be frustrated and resist. At the least they feel ambivalent. The relatively few people who welcome turning back the clock in this way probably never wanted to disrupt childhood in the first place. This was their preferred life-style, either by active choice or passive default. The younger person may not feel that he or she has sufficient psychological stamina to stand alone, or a parent meets his or her own emotional needs to control or to be adored by perpetuating the childhood dimension of the adult child's life.

Far more frequently the adult child, the parents, or both do not prefer re-parenting but feel that it is the only or most obvious way of meeting a situation of need. The ways in which they work out their definitions of their situation, the openness with which they communicate their feelings about the new arrangements, and the self-awareness they have about meeting their own needs will determine how long the new dependence will last and the extent of the emotional fallout after the arrangement is no longer necessary.

Resistance of the Adult Child to Re-parenting

Some adult children are willing and able to put their resistance to re-parenting into words, even with affection and appreciation. Others may find verbalization very difficult and act out their feelings, a somewhat less helpful response because the messages are often mixed, reducing the chance of constructive dialogue. The least productive response is to cover up strong feelings, to conceal responses, making any dialogue impossible.

In a very helpful, small book on parental response to a divorced child, Harold Smith points to a gamut of possible ways in which an adult child resists the return to dependence, especially the parent's attempt to work out the situation by giving fatherly or motherly advice.[3] Some adult children faced with what they perceive as re-parenting are unable to make a constructive response, say nothing, but are filled with silent, inward resentment. Others may become defensive because of their vulnerability in the situation. Argumentative and uncooperative, they revert to the ambivalent dependence of adolescence.

Still others become overtly hostile, verbalizing or acting out the real anger they feel at having been defeated as adults and needing to retreat into dependence. Because this reaction often produces a hostile response from the parents, who feel very unappreciated, it can trigger a deterioration of relationships. Still other adult children will avoid confrontation, finding excuses not to talk about their feelings or those of their parents.

Resistance to renewed dependence is the adult child's desperate, and often unsuccessful, attempt to preserve a measure of autonomy in a situation that does not support autonomy. Middle-aged parents experience the resistance as rejection and ingratitude. Unless they all are able to respond to the new situation creatively or to seek help in coping with it, the family members will feel trapped by the situation or by the feelings elicited by the changed circumstances.

In a society that clearly values independence, it is understandable that anger and hostility, often unexpressed, accompany renewed dependence. Society understands and accepts dependence in childhood without negative evaluation, but to the older child society sends the message that adult dependence arises from weakness and inadequacy. So the person made dependent by changing circumstances is put in a double bind; he or she needs help but is negatively judged because of that need. The situation reminds all involved that the one who helps controls the one who is helped. The situation may "push the buttons" of old adolescent struggles for power, producing an escalation of anger that feeds on itself.

The Return of the Divorced Child

In our day probably the most common circumstance for the return of some dependence is the return of the divorced child. We focus upon it here as a way of understanding the phenomenon of the empty nest revisited. This return to the nest is constituted by not only a possible physical return to the parental home but, alternatively, by a renewed emotional or financial dependence, or by any combination of these.

Restructuring Emotional Involvements

The most important changes that have taken place in the lives of the middle-aged parents and the adult child are emotional ones. They experienced growing away from each other as the child was launched, lived through a period of time between the launching and the return, and now face emotional response to the present circumstances.

The fact that the child's marriage was subjected to sufficient stress to come apart triggers emotional reactions from the middle-aged parents. They may not have been aware of serious difficulty in the marriage, or they may have questioned the health of the marriage from its inception. Some parents may be deeply disappointed that the marriage has not prospered; others may be relieved that it ended.

A negative emotional reaction of the parents to the divorce profoundly affects their relationship with their adult child. They may be ashamed of the failure of this marriage and fear losing face in the community. As more and more families experience the divorces of their children, however, the social stigma is greatly lessened. Nevertheless, any feelings of shame or embarrassment provide a test of parents' willingness to stand by their children, even in the face of social pressures.

Because society expects parents to communicate values to the younger generation, any failure of that generation is often seen as a reflection on the parents. A good marriage for their children and the establishment of a new home with grandchildren delineates—for many—successful parenting by the middle aged. When that does not happen, it can be seen to represent a failure of both the adult child and the parents. While this may not be the first time that parents have faced the question "Can I be comfortable with my child's failure?" it can prove to be one of the most difficult of such times.

A common way that parents handle society's judgment on their child's marital failure is to put all or most of the blame on the in-laws, at least in public; or in an even more pointed attempt to demonstrate that they are in no way at fault, some parents will add, "If only you had listened to us in the first place!" If parents feel threatened, either by community disapproval or by the inability of their child to make a successful marriage, they may become defensive. The usual consequence of such a reaction is to try to get back into control, to re-parent.

The Temptation to Re-Parent the Divorced

While the invitation, implicit or explicit, to "come back home again, and we'll pick up where things were when you left" may be well intentioned on the part of the parents and may even be welcomed by a desperate adult child, the sentiment is an impossible dream. We often hear Robert Frost's definition: "Home is the place where, when you have to go there, they have to take you in" ("The Death of a Hired Man"). While there is truth in those words, we must acknowledge that they say absolutely nothing about *how* you are taken in. That is the key. Very few parents would find it in their hearts to turn out the lights and lock the door when they find an adult child wanting or needing to revisit the empty nest. But there are many possible responses to such a situation, some constructive and some destructive. These responses can be characterized by the style of the relationships in the nest revisited, whatever form that revisiting may take.

Sometimes parents assume they can go back to the way things were in the parent-child relationship when the child left the parental home, with all the overtones of parental authority, control, and split-level communication. They may totally ignore the passage of several years, disregarding the experiences of the adult child as a spouse and, perhaps, as a mother or father.

The alternative is for parents to acknowledge that this is the return of an *adult* child who is experiencing a crisis, a child who has had some years of relative independence in which there have been significant learnings. If parents can see the possibilities of an interdependent relationship, they can communicate on an adult level to an adult and take into account the development of the son or daughter since the launching. The patterns of the former parent-child relationship will not be uncritically resumed. However, most people do not slip into this constructive mode automatically. It requires serious intent.

Readjusting is complicated by the failure of the child's marriage and the collapse of the new home. The sortie into adult independence didn't work out. Because they have been turned to for help in this crisis, some parents are tempted to try to control their adult child's life. It is a natural tendency for many people to enjoy the role of "rescuer." It may be a source of ego support for a parent to feel needed by someone. The parents may see the rescue as a confirmation of superior wisdom or strength to deal with a crisis. Parental "Lone Rangers" are not necessarily a vanishing breed.

Other parents prefer to be asked for help. In some instances, it is admirable when parents don't rush in to assist before help is requested, because it may reflect recognition that their child will ask for the help that is needed only to supplement his or her own resources. But in other instances, waiting to be asked before they offer help allows parents to require the surrender of the adult child, to admit that he or she cannot handle the problem alone; it is an assertion of control by the parents.

The failure of the adult child's marriage may be interpreted by parents as a vindication of their wisdom or judgment, especially if they had expressed their disapproval forcefully before the marriage and had not been heeded. So the former parental role of values instructor is invoked, and the lesson plan is put into effect once again: "Let us guide you again, until you get it right."

If there are children, the break-up of a marriage means a massive dislocation. Some middle-aged grandparents panic. Their desire to help their child in a situation they interpret as desperate causes them to declare a state of emergency. This entitles them to assume control over the situation, to get it sorted out and on the way to recovery.

Other parents may not have a strong need to control in this overt way. They may be moved to help because they sympathize with the hurt of their child whose marriage has failed. As overly protective parents they may have taken their child's side against teachers or aggressive playmates. Their identification with the pain of their adult child in marital crisis gets all those old juices flowing, and they rally to their child's support. With good intentions they limit their adult child by fostering renewed dependence in greater measure than required by the situation. The approach, as in earlier years, is to subtly control the child by controlling his or her environment.

All of these controlling measures will be met with subtle or not so subtle resistance by most adult children. A few may welcome the return to the total security of a warm, fuzzy parental relationship. But most adult children, having had the experience of independence, will not accept regression to dependence and parental control gladly. The middle-aged parents, trying to re-parent to help a difficult situation, may experience this reluctance as rebellion and rejection. They are trying to help, and their adult child, who has not had a lot of success lately in managing his or her life, is foolishly or stubbornly resisting their help.

Very often everyone feels a great deal of ambivalence. The parents struggle over the best way to provide help. The adult child both recognizes the need for help and fears the control that it implies. Smith describes such a situation: "'I'm damned if I do, damned if I don't' one parent admitted in anguish. 'I wish I knew where I stood. One day she wants my help, the next day she doesn't. I never know which mood she is going to be in.'"[4]

Rather than seeing re-parenting as a return to former modes of relating a dependent child to parental authorities, it is much more productive to see re-parenting in a new way. It can be an adult-to-adult relationship, which preserves individual freedom as much as possible. The parents have the freedom to offer help, and the adult child has the freedom to accept as much or as little as he or she wishes. These are not necessarily fixed positions but can be negotiated between adults. Much value lies in thus enabling the growth of persons within the interdependence of the family system. Interdependence implies boundaries between persons. Relational boundaries engender freedom, responsibility, and selfhood for each family member.

Moving in with Parents

The physical return to the nest is often contingent upon the housing arrangement of the divorced adult child. The couple had a home in which only one of them could continue to live; the other spouse had to find new accommodations. In a marriage without children, either of the spouses or both might move out of the home. When there are children, it is more likely that custody arrangements will allow the wife to retain the home—if the couple can afford it—and the divorced husband will move out. So it is that a larger proportion of divorced or separated men than women return to the home of origin.

Studies also show that the younger the divorced person, the more likely he or she is to return to the family home. Paul Glick and Sung-Ling Lin report on the proportion of separated or divorced persons twenty to thirty-four years of age who were living in the homes of relatives in 1984.

> From a crest of fully 40% for those 20–24 years of age, the proportion of separated and divorced persons living with relatives dropped sharply to 23% for those in the next older age group, 25–29, and to 17% for those 30–34.[5]

This suggests that the longer the adult child experiences independence, the less likely he or she is to return to the nest, and that the longer the person has experienced independence, the more uncomfortable is the return.

If the adult child is the custodial parent, there may be child-care responsibilities for the middle-aged grandparents. If there is a physical return to the nest, such responsibility may be major. Even if the adult child maintains his or her own home, child care during working hours may be necessary. Grandparents may furnish child care or help to pay for it.

Grandparents are viewed by some as a feature of Currier and Ives nostalgia, with homes full of smells of grandma's apple pie and merry elderly men telling stories in rocking chairs. In present reality not everyone entertains those romantic notions about middle-aged grandparents. Some are characterized as overindulgent spoilers of the young or as strict, critical authoritarians; in either instance, as competitors with their adult children-parents. Still, many grandparental relationships are loving, supportive, and noncompetitive.

In a very disruptive time in the life of the dissolving family, grandparents may be a major stable component of the family system. In the return to the nest of the divorced adult child with his or her own children, the role of the grandparents will probably be that of surrogates, taking over major parental responsibilities when parents cannot fulfill that role. The dependence of the adult child very often includes a similar dependence of the grandchildren.

One of the most important functions for grandparents under such circumstances is to provide emotional support. People who do not verbalize easily may convey their support with gifts and by spending time with the child. In enabling the grandchild to talk about how he or she feels in this time of turmoil, the grandparent offers a major opportunity for reassuring the child of caring support. Even though the grandparents may have strong alliances with one parent and equally strong dislikes for the other, they can try to explain to the child what is happening and support the relationships of the child with both parents.

Children should not be put in the position of having to take sides in the contention between their parents. At all costs, children should not be used as weapons in the conflict between divorcing spouses or between generations. Grandparents who consciously or unconsciously feel angry at their former son- or daughter-in-law, or who are defensively holding that person responsible for the break-up of the marriage, may be tempted to convey their anger or reproach to their grandchildren.

Adults need to listen very carefully for children's statements implying that they may somehow be at fault for the collapse of their home. Children, up to and including adolescents, often have tortuous misunderstandings of cause and effect chains, sometimes assuming that they bring misfortune on themselves and others. Communicating love to children, by whatever means are most available and in ways in which one is most comfortable, is the major task of the grandparent in such a situation.

Re-parenting Through Financial Dependence

Financial independence marks adulthood most clearly in our society. To have to seek sustained financial support from parents means for many regressing to childhood. It is quite acceptable for children to borrow from parents to make large purchases or even to receive as a loan or gift the downpayment for a home. But having parents provide for the adult child's day-to-day expenses meets with far less social approval.

We also recognize that the present social outlook often presents money as the answer to all problems. When money is seen as an oversimplified solution, it becomes a way of avoiding the problem. Throwing money at a problem distances us from it; it helps us avoid more constructive involvement. So, in one sense, financial support for an adult child in difficulty can be a way we avoid wider involvement.

On the other hand, in our society money commandingly symbolizes power. The one who pays the bills is in control. Because control stirs up intergenerational tensions in a return to dependence, the way in which financial aid is given and received is crucial. Sometimes people are more comfortable construing financial assistance as a loan. The implication is that this is a business arrangement between adults and that the money will ultimately be returned to the lender with interest. It cannot be seen as a handout. But such an understanding is possible only if that is *truly* the arrangement. If "loan" is a euphemism for financial support and the parties know that repayment will never take place (either because it is impossible under the circumstances or the intention is lacking) the "borrower" may have a greater sense of guilt than if he or she simply accepted financial aid. Any strings that are attached to the financial assistance should be clearly understood.

If the middle-aged parents assume that supporting, temporarily or on a sustained basis, their adult child and, perhaps, grandchildren, gives them the right to be the major participant in all decisions, friction is almost inevitable. It is demeaning for an adult child to be reduced to the status of adolescent because of the need to be financially dependent. At the same time, the middle-aged parents whose support for their adult child is provided at some sacrifice may see the finances mismanaged or unproductively used. How serious that problem becomes depends very much on the level of communication. If both parties can share their feelings freely and constructively and can receive them in this way, the arrangements can be workable.

Some middle-aged parents are put in a financial bind by the return to dependence of an adult child, especially if they also confront financial needs in their aging parents. Our society had assumed that in the later years of life parents would need some help from their middle-aged children, who at that time would be at their maximum earning level. It was also assumed that young adult children would by then be financially independent, freeing resources of the middle aged to deal with the needs of elderly parents. A generation may be caught in the middle, confronting financial dependency in both the younger and the older generation.

Dating and Remarriage

One of the areas in which control may be involved is in the social relationships of the divorced adult child. An arena for a return to the values struggle of adolescence, when dating and mate selection were major issues, may command attention.

Especially if there is a physical return to the nest, but certainly not limited to that development, the adult child who returns to dependence often represents a life-style of his or her own generation, rather than that of the parents. This can create stressful relations. Just as they were with the adolescent, parents are often concerned about whom their child is seeing, what he or she does, and when the child comes home. But now the parents are dealing with an adult child.

As in adolescence, much of the values tension between generations focuses on sexuality. Many divorced adult children, after the initial numbing disillusionment, want to resume normal adult social relationships, which certainly include dating. When the empty nest has been revisited, parents sometimes find themselves in a dilemma. On the one hand, they want their adult child to remarry, to find happiness with a new mate. They welcome the dating as an avenue to that possibility. On the other hand, they are aware that the values of the younger generation permit and support a sexual relationship as part of serious dating. So parents' support of dating also has the effect of legitimizing sexual relationships outside of marriage. This is one of the areas where the parents' need for or assumption of the right to control is tested.

Parents may recognize the danger of their divorced child's marrying on the rebound. Or they may feel their adult child is repeating some of the same mistakes in mate selection and style of relating that brought an end to the first marriage. They face the choice of simply biting their lips and remaining disengaged or of attempting to control the outcome of the new relationship. Neither option is desirable. Again, adult to adult communication occasions the best response. Such communication conveys support while at the same time enables the young adult to think through and talk through the decisions being made. However, if underlying the discussion is the implication of parental control, it will prove less fruitful.

Where Is the Church in This?

In the situation of the adult child's parental dependence, the concern of the church for the positive growth of persons could be expressed by this question: "How can parents and adult children turn a regressive situation into a springboard for growth?"

The term "growing in grace" has been part of Christian vocabulary from its very beginning. That phrase contains several rich meanings. All growth involves grace, undeserved gifts. Just as our bodies cannot grow without receiving nourishment, our lives do not simply grow out of our own personal resources. We receive countless supportive contributions that enable us to become who we are. These are really gifts. We do not have to earn them; we do not seize them.

Christians recognize how basic the *quality* of giving and receiving is in a person's return to dependence. The following questions demand a personal response from us: Does giving symbolize power and control, while receiving represents weakness and inadequacy? Do giving and receiving have conditions attached to them?

Theologically, we understand that what we have to give is not something that is an absolute possession of ours. It is something that we have received, whether we think of it as a gift of Divine Providence or, in more mundane fashion, as the result of others helping us along our way. Although the so-called Protestant ethic interprets affluence or possessions as a mark of God's favor—with the corollary that poverty or need is a likely indicator of divine displeasure—the mainstream of Christian theology stands over against such self-serving interpretation. What we give is in a real sense always something with which we have been gifted. So to use it as an instrument for controlling others is theologically questionable.

In the same way, the idea of grace has a lot to say about receiving as well. It makes very clear that the status of recipient is not demeaning but is an indicator of being valued. Although the theological meaning of the line "that saved a wretch like me" (from the hymn "Amazing Grace") is clear, isn't the use of the word "wretch" demeaning? While it does mean "undeserving," which is probably what the hymn writer intended, it also suggests that the receiver of amazing grace is worthless. Nothing could be further from the meaning of grace. Grace communicates value, not worthlessness.

Communicating this theological principle, not necessarily only in formal teaching, but also in a quality of relationship, is an important issue for the practical pastoral caring of the church. Part of the meaning of grace is that people are loved for themselves, as they are, not as they ought to be. We are spared the tyranny of perfection, the demand to be without limitation. The reality of being finite has to be faced, but facing it isn't easy. On the one hand, we are tempted to make excuses to avoid feeling any responsibility. On the other, we are tempted to despair: "I am a failure. I really messed things up." Grace, undeserved love, values a person for being, not for being successful. It makes excuses unnecessary, and it neutralizes the despair of failure.

This theme of grace, central to the mission of the church, is very appropriate to the return to dependence, which points to failure on the part of everyone. Grace looks for ways to affirm that adult children and middle-aged parents are loved for themselves, not for independence, not for happy homes, not for perfect relationships—but for themselves.

A related task of the church is healing. The situation we have been describing is full of hurt, disruption, anger, disillusionment, loss. The entire family system, all generations, is wracked by these pains. The church's concern is not limited to deadening the pain but wants to heal the source of the pain. The church needs to encourage people to face stressful situations and work through them in constructive ways. This process is severely impeded if the approach chosen by the Christian middle-aged parents or by the adult child is vengeful or judgmental. Although wrongs produced the break-up of a marriage and family and brought about the death of a once meaningful relationship, the responsibility for these wrongs is broadly shared, rather than falling on the head of one person. While wallowing in a sense of guilt is not usually helpful, neither is claiming no part in the fault a means to growth.

This brings us again to "growing in grace." The complexities of life and of our own selves are such that we simply cannot live without making mistakes, often serious mistakes with painful consequences for ourselves and others. This is the cost of living in an interdependent network with other people who are as imperfect as we are. The church's presentation of grace, in both the divine and human sense, does not relieve us from the responsibility to try our best but does relieve us from the pain of knowing that our best is never good enough. When people are in situations that have "failure" branded on them, the church's message to live as "grace-fully" as possible proffers a powerful remedy.

Since we share in both the problem and the healing, interdependence remains the most constructive relational style. The church can do some very practical things to foster and empower interdependence. It can form support groups to help people in growing toward self-understanding and in working on their problems. These groups affirm the value of those with problems and sustain them in changing the things that can be changed and in accepting the things that cannot be changed.

The church can provide pastoral counseling to help people work through the complex, knotty relational problems that make life difficult. Often counseling opens communication between people who are having a hard time getting along with each other.

The church can also address, often in an advocacy role, ways to meet particular needs. For example, most communities desperately need child-care services, especially important for single parents and working mothers. A church or group of churches can press the public sector to provide such services or can provide child-care programs themselves. All such activities by the church address issues rising out of the nest revisited, providing pastoral caring in the fullest sense of the word.

Chapter 5

Caring for the Older Generation

For a variety of reasons American society does not feel at ease with aged persons. It has been suggested that an almost neurotic denial of death has spilled over into a denial of aging, the ultimate terminal condition. We so associate independence with the good life that we dread circumstances in which we will become increasingly dependent. This dread causes us, consciously or unconsciously, to fear the deterioration and the humiliation of growing dependence that inevitably accompany old age.

The needs of the elderly have broad political implications in our time. The growing number of persons over age sixty-five make them a political force, which impacts on the national economy. It is estimated that by the year 2040 20 percent of the U.S. population will be sixty-five and older and 40 percent of the federal budget will go to their support. Many in the younger generation are beginning to feel this as a growing threat.

The socially supported bias against growing old becomes a hidden feature of the attitudes of both middle-aged children and their aging parents. The children feel imposed upon by the need to help their parents, and the parents feel humiliated by the need for that help. How different this is from those cultures or times in which the aged were venerated for their long lives, and when their long experience was regarded as wisdom. Then their growing dependence, viewed positively, enabled a reciprocity for their years of caring for dependent children!

The cultural bias against growing old has given rise to a number of erroneous assumptions. Older persons are believed to be rigidly opposed to change, to have very diminished mental power, to be only fractional persons in the later years of their lives. While it is true that some older persons, because of significant physical problems, do experience a diminution of some of their faculties, this is not the case with all elderly. However, the case for the sustained powers of the elderly must not be so strong that it reenforces the youth cult of our era. If we only value older people who look, feel, and act young, then those who have declining powers and become increasingly dependent are devalued. Books that extol the vibrancy and vitality of the elderly reveal such biases. While they intentionally point out that many older people are as active and productive as ever, they unintentionally contribute to the bias against those who cannot achieve such a goal.

In the later years many relationships, one of the stabilizing forces of life at any age, are lost. Retirement separates a person from co-workers and colleagues. The inevitable death of friends and relatives narrows the circle of contacts. The impact of the death of a spouse creates a massive loneliness and often precipitates escalating dependence. As Reuel Howe writes:

> As we grow older we are faced with losses, sufferings, failures, and deaths. All of these cause in us feelings of bereavement, that is, sorrow for what we have lost or for what has been taken from us. Some experience these losses bitterly, and never recover from them; others are able to relinquish what is gone with an acceptance of the loss and a treasuring of the meaning of what had been a cherished part of their lives. These latter persons are able to find compensations which they pursue with interest and hope.[1]

Although one applauds Howe's capacity for gaining perspective and transcending limitation, there is a kind of implicit triumphalism here. It assumes that much of what happens to a person is due to his or her own attitudes and decisions. This is partially true, and his conclusions are valid there. But what of the impact of circumstances beyond a person's control, physical and social? Is this not somewhat akin to the belief that the poor deserve what they get because they do not pull themselves up by their own bootstraps? This is certainly not what Howe intends, but there is a danger that positions like his will be understood that way.

The Family and Responsibility

E. Brody observed that it is ironic that, for the "empty nest cohort" (women aged fifty to sixty), the empty nest is being filled with grandparents.[2] The normal expectation is that during their lifetimes people will establish a network of social relationships beyond the family. However, when illness, loneliness, disability, or poverty creates a need for a return to dependence, this network usually shrinks drastically. Only infrequently do persons outside the immediate family provide care for the elderly, except in the case of those who purchase care through a retirement community or nursing home. An examination of the care of the elderly generation found that, with only very occasional exceptions, family care is provided almost entirely by middle-aged children and children-in-law, not by elderly siblings or grandchildren (although economic support may be shared).

Ethel Shanas, who interviewed more than thirty-six hundred elderly people in five countries, found that 80 percent of the elderly visited frequently with one or more children.[3] This familial social and psychological support did not depend on distance so much as on social and psychological compatibility; for example, similar educational levels or similar social class expectations strengthened bonds. This would help to account for stronger intergenerational support systems in blue collar society than in white collar society.

However, impediments to strong intergenerational relationships exist, particularly when these involve caregiving. In a time when most adult children, including middle-aged women, are employed outside the home, claims for caregiving by elderly parents compete with claims of the workplace, the family budget, energy, and time.

Although to reduce caregiving needs to business terms may seen insensitive, a cost-benefit ratio consideration emerges sometimes in the decision-making involved in meeting the needs of elderly parents. As the elderly become increasingly dependent because of illness, shrinking financial resources, or inability to care for themselves, their familial caregivers weigh the cost of such care against benefits that they derive. The costs are not only monetary but include time, energy, and emotional involvement. The benefits, beyond the obvious improvement in the care of the elderly parent, are a deepened opportunity for relationship across the generations and the conservation of the parents' estate. Some families are more conscious of the cost-benefit ratio than others.

> Johnson and Bursk in a study of 54 pairs of older parents and their children . . . in Boston, found that the better the health, finances, attitude toward aging, and living environment of the parents, the better were their relationships with their children.[4]

The converse is that once parental needs grow, strains begin to appear in the parents' relationships with their adult children. This means that a shift in the cost-benefit ratio, with cost increasing more than benefit, adversely affects the relationship.

The Emotional Qualities of Family Relationships

Ambivalence, mixed feelings, probably most accurately characterizes the complex emotions of parent-child relationships. All of us know from experience the blending of feelings of gratitude and guilt, love and anger, freewill giving and grudging obligation, struggles for independence and needs to be dependent aroused by our families. Such feelings vary from person to person, from situation to situation. Mixed feelings are difficult to deal with. Pulled in two directions, we prefer to acknowledge the positive side of the tensions but must recognize also the claims of the negative dimension.

Responding to ambivalence felt by other people proves just as difficult. Which emotions should be acknowledged? For example, some elderly parents simultaneously want to be independent and also complain of neglect by their children; they want and need affection and care, while at the same time they fear that their children are interfering with their lives. Such complex feelings send out mixed messages and produce equally mixed responses.

Ambivalent feelings also characterize adult children's responses to their elderly parents. Eda LeShan cites as an example the feelings of a woman who said:

> I am sure that when I am eighty or eighty-five, I will struggle for my own life, and want every bit of it that I can have, but from where I sit now, I sometimes feel it's unnatural for so many people to be living so long. . . . I'm sixty-five, both my parents are still alive and their demands on me are tremendous. I constantly have the feeling that I'm a bad child because I can't make them young and happy again.[5]

Note the very strong mixed feelings of frustration, guilt, love, responsibility, gratitude, and resentment. Experienced counselors know that the best way to respond to ambivalence is to acknowledge that the person experiences a pull in two directions, rather than just responding to the half of the tension with which the person is most comfortable.

The emotional reactions in middle-aged child and elderly parent relationships sometimes grow out of the role shifts that occur with a return to parents' dependence. In early life the child was highly dependent on the parent. For some this dependence continued into young adulthood and adulthood, exaggerated by the increased life span of parents, so that the adult child feels that he or she is still in the child's role. For others a relative balancing of autonomy in both young adult child and parents followed childhood dependence. The later years of life present to older parents and adult children a role reversal, with elderly parents in the status of dependents.

This new role pattern creates a variety of dislocations. The growing infirmity of parents, symbols of strength for a lifetime, troubles both the parent and the adult child. In families that developed strong authoritarian patterns with little attention paid to interdependence, role reversal is loaded with feeling. Some find that they cannot make the shift because their own self-understandings are so closely tied to the old pattern; they cannot comfortably function in the reversed role. Some who reacted negatively to their former dependent state within an authoritarian family are tempted to turn the tables and play the rigid authoritarian themselves. Still others who are able to function in the interdependent mode of a less authoritarian family find that the required adjustments are not difficult.

Strong social conditioning creates an awareness of our duties of loyalty and caregiving within the family. These duties persist in spite of the passage of time or the intervening of distance. We should not, however, confuse this sense of obligation with a high quality of relationship. In fact, surprisingly, the less strongly obligation is felt, the better the relationship between many middle-aged children and the elderly parents. J.M. Kreps suggests that the improved financial situation of many elderly parents through pensions and Social Security benefits has decreased their economic dependence on their middle-aged children.[6] Financial security fosters interdependence and improved relationships between the generations. Although the following is not meant to be as cynical as it sounds, Streib and Beck write: "The handling of the older person's assets, and the anticipation of their transfer, may have important implications for the quality of life in the older person's last decade."[7]

Adjusting to Change

Sometimes the return to dependence by elderly parents develops suddenly. A heart attack or stroke makes it very difficult for the parent to take care of himself or herself; the death of one of the parents leaves the other very lonely, faced with unaccustomed responsibilities. Middle-aged children may have to respond very quickly to such crises.

In other families the return to dependence occurs gradually. In fact, some elderly parents who become increasingly dependent long before dependence is necessary do so from an internal need for being dependent rather than because of external crises. They avoid decisions and try to pass the decisions to their children. They default in taking responsibilities; things do not get done unless the child steps in to do them. If the adult child accedes prematurely to the implicit or explicit demands to take over, dependence can become very unhealthy, because it is motivated not so much by the requirements of external circumstances but by a poor self-image in the elderly parent. Taking over prematurely for the parent with low self-esteem only reenforces that pattern and accelerates the dependence. Much as in the early years of the parent-child relationship, appropriate timing and measured response are keys. Too much too soon, as well as too little too late, are dysfunctional reactions.

Some of the problems of a recurring need for support diminish if, instead of a simple independence-dependence equation, the mode of interdependence has been acknowledged within a family system. If persons have a picture of themselves *as both givers and receivers,* shifting patterns of need do not require them to drastically adjust. Such patterns cause most distress to those who had assumed that they were self-sufficient or who had revelled in the illusion of their freedom from responsibility.

Sometimes interdependence reflects the working out of a sequence of giving and receiving over a period of many years. It does not refer only to a simultaneous giving and receiving: "I give you this; you give me that." Because it involves a developmental process, a person may give more in one period of life than he or she receives, and vice versa.

The most positive consequence of such interdependence is the effect it has on persons involved, rather than the helpful things done for one another. It acknowledges and confirms them as valuable because they *are* something, not because they *do* something. The elderly are not reduced to being passive recipients of the charity of others, no matter how cheerfully given. The elderly have their own responsibilities to fulfill in the interdependent family system.

Where to Live?

One of the things that makes us real persons is that we take up space; there is a place where we live. The living arrangements of elderly people, then, have two functions: to provide a comfortable place to live and to provide emotional nurture and support for their selfhood.

Although both parents and children may recognize that where they live will someday be a problem, the decision to make a change in living arrangements is often precipitated by a major crisis in the life of elderly parents. Until such a crisis many elderly parents maintain their own homes. Unlike some other cultures, our culture places high value on adults establishing their own homes, particularly when married. So the message sent by our society is that people should maintain their own homes as long as possible and that alternate living arrangements are avenues to drastically reduced independence, curtailed personal privacy, and diminished self-esteem.

The three most common alternative living arrangements for older adults are these: moving into the home of the middle generation, becoming part of a retirement community, and being admitted to a nursing home. Although all of these mean that the persons give up their own homes, the circumstances of the new living arrangements are quite different among these alternatives. But in all three, the elderly must dispose of many possessions. Properly understood, possessions are extensions of the self, so in divesting of artifacts and memorabilia, whether of any monetary value of not, the person gives up some of the supports of selfhood. Doing so cannot be taken lightly. Those who undertake such a major shift in living arrangements, either as middle-aged children or elderly parents, must recognize that as much attention should be given to what is being left behind as to what lies before.

Living with Middle-Aged Children

Because the nuclear family rather than the extended family is a reality for a large segment of our population, with occasional and somewhat temporary exceptions, each generation tends to feel that its home is its own turf and that territorial privacy should be respected. Only when elderly parents no longer can maintain their own independent living arrangements, do most families face the possibility of a household's including two adult generations. For most families, especially in the middle class, dependent living means giving up of the value of autonomy, which has been the rule of their lives for decades.

Studies estimated that about 80 percent of elderly persons have some relatives living nearby. Of those who are not part of the minority living in institutions, nearly half are actually living with relatives. This would seem to indicate that many families are able to moderate the situation by arranging for the elderly to live nearby without being under the same roof. In Pennsylvania Dutch country, the centuries-old Amish farmhouses often have two parts. Immediately adjacent to the large farmhouse is a smaller house, the *Grossvaterhaus*, grandfather house. As the generations age, the older parents or parent moves to the smaller house, making way for the middle-aged son and his family to occupy the big house. Two households continue to exist for as long as possible, but highly interdependent. The only equivalent arrangement modern society has is a small apartment near the home of the middle-aged son or daughter.

A number of features of present-day living patterns make joint households less feasible than in past generations. A sizable portion of society is highly mobile, with the generations separated by hundreds of miles. Middle-aged couples may live in houses that do not have a great deal of extra space, or they live in apartments that are comfortable for two but confining for a larger household. Contemporary life-styles also pose problems for many families who must consider an intergenerational household. Because most women are employed full time or part time outside the home, it is the exception to have a middle-aged daughter or daughter-in-law able to provide care or supervision in the home for elderly parents. The correlation between an above average educational or economic level and employment of middle-aged women is high. For this group, leisure activities would likely involve travel, an active social life, and vacations, any of which would interfere with direct care for elderly parents in a two generation household.

Gary Lee cites Ethel Shanas' phrase "intimacy at a distance" to describe a preferred attitude of both elderly parents and middle-aged children.[8] In the best of both worlds, they live nearby but not together, offering both care and freedom. Shanas suggests that the improved economic situation of many elderly persons with pensions and Social Security income makes possible this family configuration. Elderly can afford their own living arrangements near a middle-aged child or other relative, feeling close without actually sharing space.

A fascinating study by Ishmael Okraku reports on a decade of research showing changing attitudes toward elderly parents living with their adult children. Okraku breaks this study of attitudes into decade cohorts, that is, people 20–29, 30–39, etc., to 70 +. A comparison of 1973 attitudes with those of 1983 indicates some trends.[9]

Okraku's survey showed a lot of support for intimacy at a distance: frequent contact, preferably face-to-face, but with people not living under the same roof. All generational cohorts strongly affirmed the values of independence, privacy, and the avoidance of potential conflict situations.

But when the cohorts were asked directly their attitudes toward parents living with their middle-aged children, all cohorts approved, and the approval rate went up during the decade covered by the study. However, the approval rate rose much more significantly for the younger cohort than for the older cohorts. Young people, many of whom had not yet established their own homes, were by far the most supportive of intergenerational residence. To them it seemed a good idea.

Several researchers have probed this youthful support for intergenerational residence. The easiest explanation is that youthful enthusiasm or naiveté blinds young people to the complex problems involved in such arrangements. Others have speculated that this cohort still feels strong ties to their parents and, when projected into a distant future, feels a desire to care for them. Could such an attitude compensate for adolescent guilt over rebelliousness? Whatever its origin, the surveys clearly show that young people support intergenerational residence.

The older cohorts, the elderly themselves, generally resist the idea of intergenerational shared living until they have of necessity to move in with children. They put that condition on their approval—"only if it becomes necessary." The oldest cohort, those seventy-five or older, closest to such necessity, modify their resistance to intergenerational residence and support it.

As you might anticipate, the response of the middle generation shows the lowest approval rate. Okraku compares six surveys made between 1973 and 1983 and reports:

> In a comparison of three generations of women by Brody et al. (1984): 60 percent of the young-adult granddaughters, averaging about 23 years in age, indicated approval if the married daughter was not working, compared with 36 percent of the elderly grandmothers, whose average age was 74.3 years. Significantly, the middle group of daughters, the

most likely group of caregivers, with an average age of 49 years, showed the most disagreement.[10]

This finding indicates that those for whom the cost-benefit ratio tips heavily to the cost side are less enthusiastic about the possibility of an intergenerational household than the others.

However, the Okraku survey also shows that every group, from the most enthusiastic to the least, changed to a higher approval rate during the decade studied. He shows that between 1973 and 1983 the following responses were given to the question "Is it a good idea for elderly parents to live with adult children?"

Good idea: Changed from 31.4% to 42.9%   +11.5%
It depends: Changed from 10.8% to 14.8%   + 4.0%
(This response was volunteered by respondents. It was not on the questionnaire.)
Bad idea: Changed from 57.8% to 42.3%   −15.5%[11]

Some might interpret these figures to suggest a growth in altruism. But it is also possible to interpret them as a consequence of the improved economic and health status of many elderly. With many elderly self-sufficient until much later in life, the prospect of moving in with adult children is not immediate. Many families want to avoid institutional care for the elderly unless it is absolutely necessary. All of these factors reduce peoples' objections to intergenerational residence, except for those who bear the greatest potential cost: the daughters or daughters-in-law of elderly parents. Okraku concludes:

> There is little reason to believe that the basic values on which the idea of separate residence is founded are losing their grip in America; on the contrary, recent value changes appear to reenforce them. A more likely source of explanation appears to be the changing circumstances surrounding aging in America generally and the status of the aged individuals in particular. . . . The result is a paradoxical situation in which public sentiments are growing increasingly supportive of multi-generational residence just when the incidence of such households is declining.[12]

The quality of life in an intergenerational setting is equally crucial. Here we come again to interdependence. If interdependence expresses the basic mode for relating, life is far more positive for the elderly parent than if she or he is dependent physically, socially, or economically. Dependence causes decline of the elderly parents' morale. Interdependence means that a useful role, appropriate to the situation of the elderly person, will be established. The person is not reduced to being simply a receiver but will have a role as a giver. Giving provides affirmation for the giver, showing that he or she counts for something. This role must adequately reflect the new situation. People cannot return to the role structure of earlier home life, because everyone has changed from who they were then. Frequently, mother and daughter, or father and son must avoid the pitfall of vying for the same role as in the past and creating a dysfunctional situation.

Earlier we looked at a cost-benefit ratio in the relationships between adult children and elderly parents. For the elderly parents their level of satisfaction will hinge on whether they perceive the cost to be greater or less than the reward. In most instances, the costs are balanced by the rewards. They do have to give up their own homes, their relative independence, often many of their belongings, their privacy; in return they get care, support, security.

For middle-aged children, the rewards may include companionship after years of living apart, some limited help around the home, and additional financial resources either through a contribution to household expenses or a conservation of the parent's estate. The costs may involve modest or severe limitations on the life of the adult child because of the increased responsibility, having to spend more time at home, enduring loss of privacy in the home, and experiencing the emotional stress of competing affections and loyalties. These negatives should be recognized as subjective perceptions rather than as reflecting an objective computation of assets and liabilities. They are important and determine the satisfactions experienced by elderly persons and their adult children who live together.

Retirement Home

Retirement homes and nursing homes create surrogate families, even though family members may still be in contact with each other. When the person needs to return to dependence, instead of depending on family members, he or she purchases care from institutions and professionals who are in the business of providing this necessary and important care. It is an illusion, however, for elderly persons who are moving into a retirement community to assume that they are totally independent. They are not. They have simply made a choice that rather than being dependent on their middle-aged children, they will become increasingly dependent upon the retirement community, its facilities, and its staff.

Many retirement communities are of excellent quality, with enlightened staff and healthy programs. However, such communities, of necessity, segregate the elderly. They are then out of sight of younger generations, and reminders of aging and inevitable death are hidden from the young. Many retired people welcome the transition to such a community, particularly if they make the move before growing disabled or infirm.

One far less costly and much simpler form of such elderly care is the do-it-yourself retirement community. This refers to shared living arrangements that are occasionally worked out by small groups of older persons. Rather than trying to live alone, several older persons band together into a kind of surrogate family, share a house, share costs, and share responsibilities. In lieu of accepting care from family members, they care for one another. Although such shared living arrangements can reflect all the failures of human relatedness, they can be models of interdependence. What makes them so is the clear recognition that in shared living everyone gives and everyone receives. However, they work best if members do not have major problems or limitations. Only rarely can they accommodate the needs of someone who is seriously ill or unable to participate in the household on a relatively equal basis with the others.

One phenomenon that has begun to occur as a result of these surrogate family relationships, because they may go on for some years if people enter them early in retirement, is a shift in inheritance patterns. Moving into retirement communities usually involves the purchase of an apartment or housing unit. Only a part of this initial investment is returned to the estate of the resident after his or her death. So, in effect, the retirement community becomes one of the heirs of the elderly resident. Similarly, attorneys and probate courts are beginning to see more elderly giving legacies to geriatric peers with whom they formed friendships during long periods in surrogate family settings. Such giving patterns suggests that for these elderly, commitment to blood kin has decreased and devotion to close friends of some years in the surrogate family has intensified, a shift that may be reflected in the will of the elderly person who has lived a good many interdependent years in a surrogate family setting of a retirement community or shared living household.

Nursing Home

The nursing home is the logical extension of the retirement community. The dramatically increasing needs of the elderly person may make him or her extremely dependent and require the purchase of total care. In the 1980s only about 6 to 8 percent of the population over sixty-five receive such total institutional care.

State regulation has brought an improvement of the physical facilities and standards of care in nursing homes. Because they must demonstrate cost effectiveness, they have tended to become larger, more professionalized institutions. Both their size and the fact that most people there are quite infirm in body or mind tend to make them seem somewhat impersonal, even though they may offer excellent care.

Although the services of a nursing home are most welcome when a situation of extreme dependence cannot be met in any other way, most people confront the possibility of admission with a good deal of fear. The fear of entering a nursing home is widespread among the elderly because of what it symbolizes. Not only is it an admission of total dependence, it also is seen as a terminal move, what some have regarded as premature burial. Even though admission to a nursing home may be the rational thing to do, it is very often a psychic trauma for the whole family.

Middle-aged children fear nursing homes for their parents as well. They recognize that it means that they are giving over the care of their elderly parent completely to an institution. This is costly care, much of which is not reimbursable by insurance, and people are fearful that the cost will completely erode the financial resources of the elderly and the middle aged.

There are two somewhat conflicting realities that need to be part of our reflection on nursing home care. The first is that, in spite of the perceived total dependence that requires nursing home care, an estimated 20 to 30 percent of those in nursing homes do not really need to be there because of health or family situations. They cannot care for themselves fully, to be sure, but they do not require as much service as a nursing home provides. Either lack of community-support services to enable them to live at home with some competent visiting help or lack of information within the family has led to nursing home placement.

Second, surveys have shown that to most families, admitting the elderly to a nursing home is seen as a last resort. Brody states:

> The literature is clear: prior to institutionalization, most families have endured severe personal, social, and economic stress in attempting to avoid admission; it is typically the last, not the first resort, and the decision is made reluctantly.[13]

Some nursing homes provide excellent care. Others, unfortunately, do not. Some are little more than warehouses for the aged, effectively keeping them from community view and meeting only minimal standards for such institutions. The combined facts—that nursing homes are substitutes for direct care given by the family, that they are a fearful prospect for both elderly parents and middle-aged children, and that even those that provide good care are blighted by the reputation of those that do not—make understandable the guilt that adult children often feel when they find it necessary to admit an elderly parent to a nursing home.

Although some elderly parents may be abandoned to nursing homes by their families, generally they are not. A study by Smith and Bengston contradicts the idea that institutional care represents a failure of families to support elderly parents.

> The findings presented here suggest that the majority of elderly persons in long term institutional care are close to and involved with their families. . . . For a large number of families, institutionalization of the elderly patient resulted in a strengthening of family ties or a renewed closeness between parent and child. A major reason for the improvement of family relationships was the alleviation of strain and pressure caused by the multiple physical and/or mental problems of the parents.[14]

This suggests that if selection of the institution was carefully made, adequate physical care that the family cannot provide is purchased, and the family is freed to devote its resources to visiting the patient and providing very helpful emotional support.

Health Issues

Declining health is, then, a major precipitating factor in the return to dependence. As people grow older, the healthy bodies they took for granted gradually begin to develop limitations. Understandably this produces in the elderly a preoccupation with their bodies.

William May points to the important meanings that we give to our bodies. With our bodies we control our world, manipulating the natural and social environment. Through them we savor our world, enjoying life through our senses. They are the media through which we reveal ourselves to others. We establish all of our significant relationships as embodied persons, not as abstractions. When the body begins to be limited through declining health, the changes are not simply matters of aches and pains, diminished energy, or even endangerment of life. A person's entire life is affected, because the body is the medium through which he or she experiences life. A limitation of the body is accompanied by a proportionate reduction in the power to control life, in the capacity for enjoying life, and in the ability to share ourselves fully with others. Because in a significant sense a person *is* the body, diminishing health can cause a person to feel less worthwhile, less lovable than he or she did in good health.[15]

Some elderly face physical deterioration, others a growing limitation of their mental capacities. Mental more than physical deterioration entails dramatic loss of personhood. Familial caretaking becomes more troubled. Not only do adult children have the responsibility to care for an elderly parent, but that parent is different from the person they knew and loved in earlier life. While children may feel human compassion for the parent, now a stranger in many ways, the change in personality loosens many of the old affectionate ties.

Economic Issues

The other factor beside physical and mental deterioration that precipitates the return to dependence is economic need. Since the independence and self-sufficiency of the elderly person correlates rather directly with economic status, the person who can contribute financially to his or her own care, or who can afford to purchase caregiving services, can often assure an acceptable level of care. The person with seriously depleted assets may not have as much control over the level of care.

The economic situation of the middle-aged child is also a factor in caregiving. If a parent's financial resources are minimal, the responsibility for caregiving rests upon the middle generation. For some this constitutes a heavy burden, both economically and emotionally. There is an interesting paradox here. Mindel and Wright report:

> A substantial body of research indicates that kinship ties are more salient and more functional as a mutual aid and help network for lower and working class individuals and members of ethnic subgroups.[16]

This does not necessarily imply that affluent persons are less charitable than those with more limited means. It does mean that more affluent families are less likely to be living in an extended family situation. Often they have moved far from their families, and their life-styles take them out of their homes rather than centering them in their homes. There is a certain grace in the fact that those who are least able economically to provide for their own care very often are in a family in which such care is a natural component of the family life-style.

As indicated earlier, one of the more recent developments in the economic situation of the elderly involves the participation of the public sector. Social Security and Medicare provide benefits for most citizens; supplemental income and Medicaid assistance are available to those with special need; and the publicly funded programs through Offices of the Aging provide help for the elderly in most communities. Programs such as these are generally accepted in contemporary American society. The fact that some of these programs are called "entitlements" and are supported by contributions people have made through their work life makes them not "charity." (How unfortunate that that lovely biblical concept of charity has come to be demeaning!) The fact that many of these programs benefit almost everyone dilutes the notion that some people have to be singled out as needing help. The programs encourage interdependence rather than a return to dependence. People need not feel demeaned or insulted by being recipients of such benefits.

Where Is the Church in This?

Virtually from its very beginning the church has had in its vocabulary the word "elder." Even though the word often refers to a kind of church official, it indicates that persons are respected for their accumulated years and the wisdom they have accrued. Remembering its historical usage, even its Hebrew origins, should stimulate the church's pastoral instincts to resist situations that demean the elderly and to support those that affirm their worth.

For the aging person the church affirms the possibility of maturing and growing in grace. Even though the church acknowledges that for some aging persons health deteriorates and resources are increasingly limited, these losses must not be permitted to dehumanize them. The church's attitudes regarding its "elders" provides an important paradigm.

A major pastoral caring issue in situations of the aging is to help people deal with the guilt that seems almost unavoidable. Elderly parents, influenced by the tremendous value our society places on self-sufficiency, may feel guilty because they need to return to an increasingly dependent state. Middle-aged children may feel guilty because they cannot assume the responsibilities the situation requires. People feel guilty because they find themselves making cost-reward assessments, as if they were computing whether or not providing care was in their own best interests. Whether through pastoral counseling, support groups for middle-aged persons, or the adult education program of the church, these feelings can be addressed.

The church also has a role in innovation, in supporting new services to ease the situations of many elderly parents and their middle-aged children. One area in which the need for such services stands out is the situation of the elderly person unable to be totally self-sufficient but whose needs are not so great that he or she must enter institutional care. The church can advocate for community support services enabling people to be cared for in their own homes as long as such care is desirable and possible. Or the church may create and support community facilities that provide short periods of respite for families caring for elderly parents in their homes. These include day-care facilities for the elderly or residences to which elderly people requiring care can go for a short time while their family is on vacation or away on business. Some churches have organized drop-in centers for the elderly, sometimes with a noon meal, to provide supportive relationships and fellowship. Only as the church is sensitive to the needs of the elderly can it be responsive in advocating such needed services.

Finally, William May proposes that in addition to reminding children of the responsibility they bear toward their parents, the church needs also to remind elderly parents that they have responsibilities as well.[17] Doing so acknowledges aged persons as moral beings, even as they return to increased dependence.

It is a pastoral issue for the church that elderly persons not be deprived of their moral stature by those who assume that, like little children, the elderly are passively, not actively, involved in moral life. Regarding elderly people as interdependent affirms that they have moral responsibilities. May describes three kinds of moral duties the elderly should fulfill. They are to stand with courage in the face of decline, courage that enables them to affirm life even in the face of approaching death. They are to stand with humility. By this May means that the elderly have a moral responsibility to demonstrate that receiving is not a demeaning mode, that it is all right to receive when in need. Thus the elderly can serve a society obsessed with the prideful illusion of self-sufficiency. Third, the elderly have a moral responsibility to be patient. Being patient is not the passive response of simply drifting quietly with the current. It is an intentional response in which a person maintains control of his or her spirit, deliberately shaping personal attitudes in a period of life when declining powers make controlling other dimensions of life very difficult.[18] The pastoral caring of the church is directed to helping the older generation exercise moral leadership by accepting responsibilities and helping to guide the middle generation in the fulfillment of its responsibilities in the light of this wisdom.

Chapter 6

Confronting the Death of the Older Generation

It has been estimated that nearly twelve million Americans lose a parent through death every year. Although the passing through life of one generation after another is a natural occurence, we need to recognize that the loss of a parent is very significant because it terminates a life-long relationship. This death touches us at a very deep level because it necessitates a change of identity: all through our lives we have been someone's child, but now we are not.

Death as Disruption of the Family System

When we live in a relational network of interdependence, the death of one of the members of that network leaves a gap in the family system as well as in the life of each person in the family. If we think of this family network as woven of ropes, with each member one of the strands, then death cuts one of these. The effect on the family stability will be determined in large part by how crucial that particular strand was in the total family system. If the elderly parent who dies had lived hundreds of miles away and was seen only every few years, his or her death is rather different from that of the elderly parent who had lived in the home of the adult child or just down the street, actively participating in the family's life. When that strand of the network is cut, the whole web shifts and reconfigures.

How the survivor responds to such a loss is very much influenced by how that person experiences the disruption of the family system. Does the loss mean that the surviving child now has to become a more important part of the network, with increased responsibility for the whole? Does the loss mean that the person has lost a major anchor for his or her life and will have to struggle to find a new stability? Or does the loss mean that the child is no longer tied down by the network?

Bonding

One of the experiences that makes the death of a parent particularly important reflects a distinctive quality of the parent-child relationship. In recent years considerable attention has been given to a process that begins in the very early hours, days, and weeks of that relationship—bonding.

Both in animal and human behavior the bonding process is observable as first the mother and then, in most cases, the father develop a special relationship with the offspring and as the new baby begins to sense at a nonrational, feeling level that "I belong." Almost instinctual from the early physical contact of holding and nursing, this early, primal bonding is reinforced by socialization during the early years of life, as patterned expressions of affection, of naming, of living arrangement symbolize the child's belonging in a family. The child's personality begins to develop in relationship to the stronger persons to whom he or she is attached. This also lays the foundation for gender role development in the child.

Because bonding, the connection that insures that the infant is cared for, is essential to survival in infancy, it remains a potent experience throughout life. As the child grows to increased self-sufficiency, there continue to be strong feelings of attachment to parents. Even when dramatic, destructive disruptions occur in the parent-child relationship, this sense of attachment holds, although it may be negatively experienced.

The death of a parent brings an end to that attachment, per se, but a residue persists in memories of that parent, which have ongoing influence in the lives of the children of any age. This attachment, its dissolution, and its residue, are pivotal in the grief experience of the middle-aged child when a parent dies.

Before the Death of a Parent: Anticipatory Grief

Grief studies in the modern period have paid attention to the phenomenon of anticipatory grief—grief that occurs before clinical death actually takes place. But the understanding of the nature of anticipatory grief has changed through several decades of study.

When modern grief study began in the 1940s, a common assumption held that a person needed to do a finite amount of grief work to mourn a death. With the recognition that many people begin the grieving process well before their loved one dies came the hypothesis that, with much of their grieving done, they would not grieve much when death came.

As people became more sophisticated in their understanding of grief, they saw anticipatory grief in somewhat different ways. For example, we know that such grief remains part of the experience of those middle-aged persons who anticipate the death of a parent, either through the attrition of advanced age or as a consequence of terminal illness. But anticipatory grief is seen now to be essentially different from the grief a person experiences after the death of a loved one. This significant difference centers on the dimension of finality. The difference between anticipatory grief and grief after a loved one dies is qualitative, not quantitative. So long as the terminally ill or extremely infirm elderly parent still lives, the relationship the adult child has known has not yet completely come to an end. The residue of early bonding and some elements of personal interaction remain, even though in some cases expressed or felt in limited ways.

Some elderly parents may enjoy reasonably good health, but their middle-aged children recognize that every birthday celebration marks another year slipping into history, a subtle reminder that the remaining time is finite. Although this reminder need not become a morbid preoccupation for either the parent or the adult child, life provides a constant series of promptings of thoughts of approaching death: the deaths and funerals of friends and relatives, indications of increasing fragility, the passage of each new year. If a person is not aware of the reality of anticipatory grief, sudden feelings of depression or anxiety or stress may become troublesome because he or she does not recognize their source. Sometimes anticipatory grief expresses itself in what might be called "disproportionate grieving" for the death of the parent of a friend. By indirection, this is grief for the death of the person's own parent, which has not yet occurred.

Death of a Parent Following Extended Illness

Someone has likened the experience of being with a parent through a terminal illness or in the late stages of inexorable decline to being ground down by a glacier. The person suffers under a tremendous weight of accumulated pressure of responsibility and the painful emotional burdens of the growing crisis.

Some adult children will assume the responsibility of physically caring for an elderly parent who is dying. They have to make radical adjustments in their own lives to accommodate the tasks, even though they may have the support of home health care services or a hospice. Other adult children are unable to give the actual care themselves. The elderly parent is hospitalized or admitted to a nursing home, but the child spends a great deal of time visiting the parent to provide caring emotional support.

In either of these situations, the obligations of the middle-aged child are often so pervasive that his or her life has to be put on hold. He or she lays other responsibilities of work or family life aside and suspends personal goals, while waiting through this period of uncertainty and ambiguity. In some exceptional situations such responsibilities persist for years and have a permanent effect on the middle-aged child.

In families with several middle-aged children, the care of sick or infirm elderly parents rarely can be equitably distributed. The location of peoples' homes in relation to the location of the parent, other family responsibilities, personal health considerations, and emotional temperament may reduce the involvement of one adult child and increase the responsibility of another. This situation can easily produce stresses within the family network, whether they surface or not. It is understandable that the person providing most of the care and experiencing the major limitation would grow somewhat resentful of others who cannot or do not bear equal responsibility. Similarly, the person unable to take his or her full share of the responsibility may be troubled by feelings of guilt. Resentment and guilt become complications for their grieving.

Gender appears to play a role in the distribution of responsibility for the elderly. Our cultural conditioning often causes us to place the heaviest responsibility for care on the daughters and daughters-in-law. Male adult children tend to feel less involved, to put some emotional distance between themselves and their parent's illness. This involvement or distancing can become a factor in how they grieve for the dying or deceased parent; their grief may be influenced by their deeply missing the person and by their feeling guilt because of limited involvement.

"'The worst thing of all,' a friend told me, 'is not the financial burden, or having to spend so much time with them, or playing God making arrangements for their living. It's watching the deterioration.'"[1] It is even more difficult to watch a parent in pain or mental anguish. With both empathy and embarrassment the adult child sees the degradation of the parent, who is becoming a shadow of his or her former self, a childlike or infantile dependent.

Such a decline, as we pointed out earlier, necessarily produces a drastic role reversal. Literally as well as symbolically, the parent may revert to an infantile dependence. The weight of such an experience on the child is not simply the physical care needed, even though it may be gladly provided, but the emotional loss of the strong, providing parent. Both parent and child have experienced a great loss. At the same time the childlike parent and the parenting child may affirm a new bonding. Despite that possibility, the situation dramatically illustrates the loss of the original bonding, because the roles are reversed. The shock of that experience must not be underestimated.

Anger in Anticipatory Grief

It is understandable that many elderly parents will be resentful of the return to dependence. They experience this as a humiliation and may vent their anger and frustration on the very people who are trying to be helpful to them. Colin Murray Parkes is quoted as saying:

> Parents may feel resentful that you'd let them down, even though you didn't think you did. This is an accusation which old people sometimes make to the young out of their own sense of helplessness or fear, or out of their grief over the loss of their bodily functions, and so on. They take it out on the family.[2]

Unless one can realize that extreme frustration stirs such outbursts, a great deal of unnecessary stress may be added to an already complex situation. No easy solution exists: the dependence is real; the care is absolutely necessary. Because the very receiving of the care is often experienced as humiliating, the act of helping becomes the cause of that parent's anger. The adult child readily feels the no-win situation. The only antidote for such a poisonous situation is to understand it in the context of interdependence. It might be too much to expect a change in the parent's attitude, but the middle-aged child can change his or her attitude. The helping relationship, in spite of its frustrations, can be seen as part of an exchange for the limited contribution of the elderly parent or as restitution for the care the parent gave many years before, when the child was the dependent.

Another form of anger in anticipatory grief is heard in the familiar words of Dylan Thomas, written while his father was dying:
"Do not go gentle into that good night. . . .
Rage, rage against the dying of the light![3]
Note the language of vigorous conflict against the enemy, death. Note also that it was not the dying man who spoke, but the adult child. Here a son rages against parental death, feeling victimized by the impending loss.

Fear in Anticipatory Grief

Although the fear of death varies from person to person, several common fears may be described. The first is the fear of being without parental support. Even though they have been largely self-reliant since young adulthood, most middle-aged people still experience a shadow of parental support. It has been there for years, even if it was needed only on rare occasions. Soon it will be there no more. So, for most people, there is the fear of the loss of a possibility, fear of a kind of unsupported loneliness.

A more potent fear is that of not being able to cope with the actual process of their parent's dying. Because death presents an uncommon occasion, for which life has presented little or no prior experience, the children surviving the parent do not know how they will react. It is quite possible in our time for people to be well into middle age before they encounter death at close range in the death of their parent. This may be especially fearful for those caring for a seriously ill parent in their home. Some will frankly admit their fear, "I just don't think I can handle it."

An even more potent fear involves the dread of a person's own mortality. We have already indicated that middle age is a developmental period when people begin to confront their limitations, including their mortality. Our culture in recent generations has resisted that confrontation and exerts a mighty effort to disguise even the aging process, saying, in effect, that people will live on forever. The approaching death of a parent indicates to the middle-agers that they too are moving up in what has been called the pecking order of death. This idea of an order is a defense that most people have used from their adolescent days on: "death is a long way off; millions of people will die before my turn comes." This "actuarial defense" proves effective while people are young. Once past fifty, the odds begin to shift, and the defense is less workable. The death of a parent moves a person up in the generation chain and brings closer the day when "my turn will come."

To avoid thinking about their own death, many people develop new defenses: they bury themselves in their work to convince themselves of their indispensibility; they may try to appear to stay young or to act young; they may change mates or seek younger partners to recapture youthful sexuality. All of these and many other defenses constitute an effort to avoid facing up to mortality. For some the death of a parent collapses their defensive system; for others it stimulates the frantic search for a defense.

Holding On or Letting Go

Those who work with the terminally ill through hospice programs often speak of families giving dying patients permission to die. Family members have a choice between two attitudes: holding on to or letting go of the dying parent.

Some adult children have great difficulty facing the approaching death of their parents. For one reason or another, which varies from person to person, they cannot let a parent go—sometimes because of unfinished business in their relationship, that is, issues that must somehow be resolved before the relationship can end. Sometimes letting go seems like an act of disloyalty or abandonment. In yet other instances holding on to the parent results from trying to satisfy a need for dependence either in the parent or the adult child.

The willingness to relinquish life, to let go, does not have to mean despairing acceptance of the inevitable. For some it can be an affirming act, a recognition that life together has been good, and now with the end in sight, it is appropriate to draw the relationship to a loving closure. It is like a host graciously giving a guest permission to draw the visit to a close and to leave. Consciously engaging in the process of anticipatory grief very often leads to this kind of graceful leave-taking. So often when such permission is given, explicitly or implicitly, the terminally ill person relaxes and dies.

Wishing for the Death of a Parent

In some situations of extended terminal illness or protracted severe deterioration of body and mind, it is quite understandable that an adult child will wish for the end to come for the parent. This wish grows out of a conviction that the quality of life of the elderly parent has deteriorated so drastically that death is preferable. Such a quality assessment may be made on the basis of the parent's severe pain, loss of capacity for meaningful relationships, or inability to find satisfaction in daily existence. It may be somewhat easier to wish for the death of a parent with a short life expectancy because of rapidly advancing cancer than for a parent who is suffering the slow death of Alzheimer's disease.

In some instances wishing for death to come involves a decision to terminate heroic treatment, to disconnect life support systems, to decide against additional surgical intervention, to request that the parent not be resuscitated if his or her heart stops. But in other situations decisions may be less clear-cut. Should medications for other unrelated conditions be withdrawn? Should nutrition be withheld from a comatose patient? In other words, does a person act on the wish for death to come? These questions do not present abstract issues but emotionally laden concerns growing out of the parent-child relationship. These issues touch on all the naturally ambivalent feelings of the relationship, making the decisions highly complex and stressful.

It is difficult to wish for the death of a parent without experiencing some feelings of guilt. Such a wish seems like an abandonment, like disloyalty. Most often adult children counter this guilt feeling in two rational ways. First, they perceive the wish for death to come as being in the best interest of the elderly parent: he or she would be better off dying. Second, the adult child believes that death is what the parent wants under the circumstances. This assumption is easily accepted if the parent and child discussed earlier the possibility of such circumstances or if the parent has prepared a Living Will.

Life and death decisions present great difficulty for a family operating out of a dependence-independence model, because that model implies a decision made by the stronger, independent party on behalf of the weaker, passive, dependent person. The stronger person feels justifiably uneasy about making such a decision for the other with no participation on the latter's part. However, if a family is operating on the model of interdependence, they make such life-controlling decisions more easily. Giving and receiving involve all of the parties in the decision; *mutual* interest is more sharply focused.

After the Death of a Parent: The Grief Process

When we experience a major loss, we grieve. When a loved one dies, we feel the pain of separation. Normal functioning is difficult, because we face the task of reorganizing our lives without the presence of parents who have been significant players in our lives.

Initial Reactions

Even when death has been anticipated for some time, it comes as a shock! "It has happened"; "My father (my mother) is dead." Like the numbness that protects us from the full force of a cut or bump, the human psyche temporarily insulates itself from shock. It is very common for people to feel numb for a few hours or even a few days following the death of a loved one. Numbness serves the helpful function of allowing such shocking circumstances to enter our awareness gradually, giving us time to make adjustments, some of them painful, to life without the presence of someone who has been a meaningful part of that life.

Usually the numbness lasts only for a brief period. It is important that this be a temporary state; if it goes on and on, the grieving person cannot function effectively because of an unwillingness to face up to the reality of the loss.

As the numbness gradually fades, sadness, a common response to painful loss replaces it. The sadness intensifies as the person becomes aware of the finality of the loss. Sadness has been likened to feeling empty. It is as if something very important had vacated the person's inner self, leaving a void. Even though a parent's death had been expected, perhaps wished for, the adult child still experiences a void.

The Tasks of Grief Work

"Grief work" is the powerful term given to the process of mourning someone who has died. Mourning is, indeed, work. It requires a serious effort over many months to bring a kind of wholeness back to a life radically disrupted and changed by the death of a loved one. Six tasks need to be accomplished to recover from such a loss.

First, it is important to come to terms with the loss, both intellectually and emotionally. The death of a parent confronts us with a new reality: life without a father or a mother. The new reality refers not only to loss of physical presence but to changed emotional attachments, the complex pattern of relationship with that parent. It takes time for that new reality to come into our awareness, especially in its emotional dimensions. Sometimes our parents still seems so close that we want to reach for the phone to share some news with them. Sometimes small experiences trigger feelings toward them, love or irritation; feelings once appropriate, but no longer. Only in time do we become accustomed to the reality of parents' absence from our lives.

A second task involves dealing with the past by learning to live with memories of our deceased parent. While the day-to-day relationship we have had with a father or mother ends at death, we can still remember them and the experiences we shared. At first such memories stir a lot of pain, but gradually they no longer make us uncomfortable. The more frequently we engage in such remembering, the less discomfort we experience. Our first memories are usually highly idealized, but in time we remember some of the more negative dimensions of the parent-child relationship. These, too, need to be woven into our mental picture of what has been lost.

A third task of grief work is finding appropriate avenues for expressing our feelings about our loss. For many folks this does not come easily because of past conditioning to the notion that feelings are private and that to share them is to impose on others or to betray weakness. Regardless of society's expectation, mourners need encouragement to be themselves, to express their real feelings, to share their feelings with those they can trust to understand and care.

Very often in grief, feelings are ambivalent, mixed. Although this is true of most situations of loss, it seems especially applicable to the death of a parent. The complexity of ambivalent feelings makes them hard to deal with. How can a son or daughter be relieved when a parent dies? Doesn't that make the sadness that is being expressed hypocritcal? Some adult children will experience self-doubt: Is my sense of relief really only because I no longer have overwhelming responsibility for my increasingly dependent parent or is it because of ambivalence toward my parent?

Because we know that ambivalent feelings often express tension between positive and negative feelings, love and hate, altruism and self-interest, they will produce feelings of regret and guilt. Theologically we assume that there is no pure good deed, but that there is always a dimension of self-centeredness in everything we do. Self-centeredness is part of being human. Caring for a parent whose health is seriously deteriorating may very well stir the best impulses in us at the same time that we are feeling very resentful because of the parent's demands on us. A sensitive person can hardly avoid feeling guilty under such conditions.

The situation is further complicated because our parent-child relationships through the years have been filled with ambivalence growing out of the natural tensions of the struggle for individuality, of authority imposed on a desire for autonomy. Many a struggle was resolved in the process of growing up or in later reflecting on that process. But any unresolved residue of such a struggle can join with the new ambivalent feelings growing out of the care of a dependent parent and increase their potency. Being able to express such feelings is the only avenue for resolving them.

The fourth task of grief work involves the building of a support system. Although intensely personal, the grief experience is not private. The support of others who stand by them in this painful time can help grieving people. One problem often encountered is that the social support system that functions so well in the first few weeks after a death demobilizes rather quickly. Because our society tends to minimize the impact of the death of an elderly parent, feeling that it is such a natural, expected event that it does not require extended adjustment, middle-aged children often do not receive more than token support for a very brief period.

The fifth task is to reorganize life without the one who has died. This involves turning from the past to the future. The first part of this task is recognition of the need for closure in the relationship with the deceased parent, that is, holding memories but acknowledging that the parent is really gone. The second part is to recognize that help comes through strengthening relationships in the community of the living. Unless the adult child was isolated for a long period by providing very intensive care for the elderly parent, he or she has a living network of family and friends. These relationships can help the grieving child to make the necessary adjustments to the loss.

The final task of grief work is finding meaning for this experience of death. Death is always a mystery, stimulating far more questions than answers. Sensitive, intelligent people want to gain a perspective for understanding something of death and its consequences. They turn to their religious faith or their philosophy of life to see what the death of their parent can mean to them. Does it signify defeat? fulfillment? judgment? Is it, so to speak, the fruit of a natural process of seedtime and harvest? Is the parent at rest? The kinds of interpretations one gives to the meaning of death affects the way in which the grief work is done, either positively or negatively.

Dimensions of Grief Unique to the Death of a Parent: Dealing with Old Dependence Patterns

Most middle-aged children have pretty well established their own independent living. They may have participated in the role reversal described earlier, with their parents becoming increasingly dependent on them. Still, when the elderly parent dies, the children find themselves yearning for that parent, reminded of the ways in which they once depended on that father or mother. So it is a symbolic dependence, rather than a real one, mourned when the parent dies. The old bonding, which dates back many decades, still has meaning. The parent lost is not only the elderly, infirm, dependent parent of recent years but the vigorous, nurturing, providing parent, who gave security many years earlier.

Occasionally there are situations where the dependence on the parent is more real than symbolic. For a variety of legitimate reasons, adult children may not have established their own independent living, so they may have more difficulty recovering from the loss of a parent than those whose dependence had become symbolic. In either instance, real or symbolic dependence, the death of the parent means that dependence has come to an end.

The Death of the First Parent

Because we have two parents, most of us confront the death of a parent twice. This book focuses on the middle years, so it will not consider the death of a parent or parents early in the life of the child. That situation has its own dynamic and special dependence patterns, which continue to have a place in later life. The relationship of an adolescent or young adult child to a surviving mother or father has unique qualities, which may exaggerate the adult child's reactions to the return to dependence on the parent's part in later life.

Also, separation or divorce may have removed one parent from the home for many years. The noncustodial parent may be almost a total stranger. While the separation may have been very traumatic and vituperative, or cordial and supportive of the child, the emotional residue of the separation will have an effect on the grief work of the adult child when the "distant parent" dies. Death finalizes the separation. Because there was not a close or affectionate relationship for many years does not mean that the surviving adult child has no adjustment to make when the parent dies. A relationship, however negative, exists to be resolved. If the relationship with the noncustodial parent has been close and supportive, only minor modifications in the normal grieving pattern we are discussing here will be felt.

The Death of the Father

Because of the importance society places on gender roles, a person has a natural tendency to have a primary identification with the parent of the same sex. The expectation is that sons will follow the role model of their fathers. Even if the father has not always provided an admirable role model, the early conditioning often continues to support a measure of respect (if not fear) of the father. When the father dies, this strong figure passes from the scene, an especially poignant moment if the father has been infirm and dependent in the final times.

Not only does the father's death deprive a son of a role model, it also produces a sense of vulnerability.

> In a recent interview, Robert Jay Lifton, a Yale University psychiatrist, explained that "When one loses a father, especially a father who has been a source of strength—and almost any father is to some degree—one then, as a son, really feels a direct line of responsibility and feels open to the world and its blows, because now one is to some strong extent one's own authority."[4]

Note that Lifton interprets the death not only as a loss but also as an opportunity. The passing of the strong father provides a chance to "become one's own authority." Although a son may have taken the step toward autonomy many years before, he may well have done so adversarially. The father's death offers a kind of permission for him to stand at last in his own strength.

Daughters will grieve the passing of their fathers' strength, but differently from sons, because there has not been the same competitive framework. In all likelihood a daughter misses a strong, nurturing father.

The Death of the Mother

Much of what was said above about gender role models also holds true for mothers and daughters. The persistence of the nurturing model for women is reflected in the fact, cited earlier, that most often daughters or daughters-in-law primarily provide care of elderly parents. It might also be valid to point out the more negative view: that social conditioning encourages women to be submissive to such responsibility even though, as we also have indicated, middle-aged women feel personally less enthusiastic than other age groups about intergenerational households.

Because the symbiosis of pregnancy, nursing, and early nurturing creates the mother-child bond, both sons and daughters feel a special sense of loss when a mother dies. Where they experience the death of a father as the loss of the symbol of security, the death of the mother represents the loss of the symbol of love and nurture. As people restructure life without the presence of one or both parents, they must somehow compensate for these losses.

Grief Shared with the Surviving Parent

Working through the death of the first parent usually means that the adult child will need to give special attention to the surviving parent. In most instances this parent, particularly in later years of life, feels intensely vulnerable because of the loss of the spouse and may become increasingly dependent upon the child. Whereas the adult children may have a broad spectrum of social resources to assist them in recovering from the loss, the elderly surviving parent finds life very constrained. As one older woman said of her adult children after her husband died, "They were good to me. But they all had their homes and families to go to. I only had an empty house."

Sometimes the sense of loss will stimulate the adult child to work toward a stronger relationship with the surviving parent, not because of increased dependency, but simply because of the preciousness of such closeness. However, sometimes the relationship to the surviving parent is increasingly strained. The strain may be the result of growing dependence or a failure by the child to empathize with the surviving parent, to appreciate how profound is the dislocation of the parent's life.

Dealing with New Dependence

Sometimes the new dependence of the surviving parent on the adult child simply displaces a long-standing dependence on the deceased spouse. Although there are exceptions, most surviving parents in the late years of life do not adopt a totally new relational style suddenly becoming autonomous, self-sufficient persons. More often an adult child is expected to take over the providing role of the deceased spouse. A significant identity question for the middle-aged child emerges: Who am I now—adult child or surrogate spouse?

This question may surface in the need to adjust the living arrangement of the surviving, dependent parent. If the elderly parent cannot take care of himself or herself, the child's family will have to assume some responsibility for that care. Death of a spouse is one of the major factors precipitating a move into the home of an adult child. This may pose special problems if a demanding parent intervenes in this way in the adult child's own marriage and family.

Other kinds of help may be required. If the death of one parent produced financial hardship, adult children may have to contribute to the support of the surviving parent, especially if he or she requires nursing home care. Even if adequate financial resources exist, the surviving parent may need help in settling the estate or in managing his or her finances. The amount of assistance given and the way in which the adult child provides it depend on a number of factors: the extent of the needs of the surviving parent, whether that parent can be reasonably self-sufficient temporarily or permanently, and the claims on the resources of the adult child.

The Death of the Second Parent

It is important to differentiate the death of the second parent from the death of the first. If the adult child has already experienced parental death, the second loss may seem to have a somewhat lesser impact. But because it is the death of the last parent, it possesses a unique thrust. It completely terminates the parent-child relationship and puts the adult child in a status he or she *never* had before: nobody's child.

The word "orphan" in our language has such a negative connotation we rarely use it today. It summons up visions of orphanages or of waifs thrown on the mercy of relatives who care for them out of a sense of family obligation. We don't like the word because it communicates extreme vulnerability and dependence.

Although a middle-aged child may have lived self-sufficiently for many years before the second parent dies, being nobody's child still communicates a strong feeling of vulnerability. The security of belonging, of being someone's son or daughter, has been an important part of the person's self-understanding for decades. Even though the adult child may not have called upon that security for many years, it was always there. Now that is no longer the case. An era has ended.

Becoming the Oldest Generation

After the death of the second parent, the adult child is no longer a child in any sense of the word. For the first time in his or her life the person belongs to the oldest generation. This transition of social status initiates a marked shift in self-understanding, an inevitable changing of the guard. A social order places certain responsibilities on people of the oldest generation. Usually they are seen as having the ultimate authority and responsibility, until they, in turn, become infirm. In this way we experience a vestige of the hereditary passing of power, at least symbolic power, as in a monarchy. While the person was a member of the middle generation, there was always someone else who symbolically had more responsibility. Occasionally this may even have produced some resentment, conscious or unconscious, because with responsibility goes power. When the person moves over to become the oldest generation, he or she finds that with the new power goes the responsibility.

For many people this new responsibility is dramatized by inheritance. At the death of the second parent, the parents' estate passes into the hands of the heirs. They now have the resources, power, and responsibility that their parents had held. Whether an estate is large or small, it is a symbol of passage into the oldest generation.

The moving into the oldest generation underlines, as nothing else does, the fact that the oldest generation dies. The transition compels in new ways the next generation to confront its own mortality. For them it is increasingly difficult to avoid the fact that movement through the generations is inevitable and inexorable.

Where Is the Church in This?

The church always is concerned to help people to cope with their own mortality. Traditionally, dealing with mortality has been thought of as preparing people to die, because Christians viewed earthly life as a kind of probationary period for eternal life. So the church in the past saw its task as guiding people to behave in certain ways, to accept certain doctrines, to make certain affirmations so that they would be "ready to die" in a state of grace.

In the present time a more existential thrust has been added to this pastoral responsibility of the church. The church sees confronting mortality as not simply a preparation for final judgment but rather as a prelude to living life now with integrity, authenticity, and fullness, because we recognize that the fleeting years precious time indeed. Awareness of the preciousness of time does not lead to a hedonistic, live-it-up attitude of "eat, drink, and be merry, for tomorrow we may die." Rather it contributes to the "Make today count!" life-style of the terminally ill person.

Caring for the bereaved has always formed an important part of the mission of the church. Earlier in this chapter the six tasks of grief work were described. It might be assumed that the pastoral caring of the church would direct itself only at the sixth task, enabling bereaved persons to find meaning in the death of a loved one. This is certainly where the traditional emphasis of the church has been. But when we understand the ministry of the church holistically, we see that the church has a concern for all six tasks of grieving.

Another role of the church is to support families who have to make life-control decisions: to continue or terminate heroic treatment, to put the dying person on or take the person off a life-support system, to give the person permission to die or rage against the dying of the light. Difficult, complex decisions, they involve not only abstract philosophical, theological, and ethical questions but also strong feelings of love, fear, loyalty, anger, and guilt. Such decisions are not to be made lightly but in a context of caring conversation for which the church can provide support.

Because of the complexity of these issues and unique individual and family circumstances, people must approach life and death decisions with flexibility. A rigid requirement on the part of the church is far less helpful than support that nurtures responsible decision making. The church should help people be well-informed so that they are able to consider all the options available to them. By considering these issues in the adult education program of the church, people can begin to grapple with them long before they face a crisis. When families are in the throes of difficult situations, the church does not decide for them but stands with them as they work through to their own decisions.

Because mourning requires dealing with the past with a kind of urgency—an era is ending—the church has a part of its pastoral caring provided a way for resolving past experience. It is impossible for any relationship to be perfect. There are going to be disruptions, tensions, even alienations, along with the positive, supportive dimensions. We almost always confront the ending of a relationship in death with some regret for things done or left undone; some feelings of guilt are practically inevitable in grief.

The church in its teaching, in its fellowship, in its worship, in its sacraments confronts the guilt that arises as an inevitable consequence of human relatedness. Whether we think in mechanical metaphors like "erasing a slate" or in more relational metaphors like "the homecoming of the prodigal," the faith of the church affirms the possibility of resolving the consequences of flawed relationships. Resolution can occur through acts of reconciliation, when possible, or through internalized acceptance of the fact that love, even retrospectively, can overcome disruption.

In addition to guilt, it is common for grieving persons to feel a good bit of anger. The frustration of a parent's long decline in health, the tremendous expenditure of emotional energy and funds in caring for the elderly during the decline, the insecurity of being left fatherless or motherless—all put mourning middle-aged children under stress. The church conveys acceptance of people as they are, even angry people, even people who may be angry at God. There is a kind of psychological healthiness in the way the writer of the psalms of lament (for example, Psalm 79), like Tevye in *Fiddler on the Roof*, could complain to God about the course life was taking.

Finally, the realization of the growth possibilities when a person becomes the oldest generation is a concern of the church. Being nobody's child and passing into the oldest generation mean that a person moves into a new phase of adulthood. Even though, like most significant changes, this change is not without trauma, it also opens a new chapter of life.

Eda LeShan sums up the idea very well:

> The death of a parent opens up new avenues of insight and perception about dependency, mortality—and immortality—the meaning of love and acceptance, the importance of remembering human frailty as well as strength—the meaning of "family"—how that includes memories and relationships that suddenly take on new and deeper significance. The

inner work of accepting and using such a separation for one's own maturation may add greatly to one's stature in middle age.[5]

There may be increased responsibilities, but there may also be increased resources. As a person sets the course for the rest of life, using as navigational points of reference memories of parents and their influence, he or she has an opportunity for growth.

Postscript

Living through the middle years can be an experience of remarkable richness. For most people it is a time of life when work becomes most rewarding, when the easier pace of life encourages enhancement of relationships, when some of the dreams that motivated earlier decades are realized.

However, as we have seen, middle age is not a period without stress. Persons cannot expect to remain on the plateau of the maximum indefinitely; decline is bound to occur. This realization stirs a time of reevaluation in which limitations have to be recognized.

In addition, for many middle-aged persons there are stresses of relationships with young adult children and elderly parents. Patterns of responsibility may shift from year to year and pose a very heavy burden on the middle-aged person. Liabilities and losses may cause others to return to earlier dependent states, creating sometimes desperate needs for assistance. But equally potent are the emotional disruptions caused by shifts in self-image, collapsed hopes, potentially degrading helplessness, and reasserted patterns of authority and power.

Solutions to the kinds of problems we have been discussing are not simple and easy. They involve profound depths within our personhood, as well as the infinite complexities of our relational networks. At times when problems seem to defy solution altogether, we can draw upon the familiar Prayer of Serenity:

> Lord, help me to change what can be changed;
> help me to accept what cannot be changed;
> help me to know the difference between them.

Notes

Chapter 1—The Years in the Middle

1. Lillian E. Troll, *Early and Middle Adulthood* (Monterey: Brooks/Cole Publishing Co., 1975), 13.
2. A number of helpful studies of middle-age personality development exist. See Gail Sheehey, *Passages* (New York: Bantam Books, 1977) and Eda LeShan, *The Wonderful Crisis of Middle Age* (New York: David McKay Co., 1975).
3. See 1 Corinthians 12:12–31.
4. Troll, *Early and Middle Adulthood*, 74–5.
5. Kyriakos S. Markides, Joanne S. Boldt, and Laura A. Ray, "Sources of Helping and Intergenerational Solidarity: A Three-Generations Study of Mexican Americans," *Journal of Gerontology* 41 (July 1986): 509–10.
6. LeShan, *The Wonderful Crisis of Middle Age*.
7. Ibid., 38.
8. Ibid., 238.

Chapter 2—Examining Our Assumptions

1. Herbert Anderson, *The Family and Pastoral Care* (Philadelphia: Fortress Press, 1984), 13–14.
2. Deuteronomy 5:16.
3. Matthew 15:1–9; Mark 7:1–13.
4. Matthew 8:22.
5. Matthew 10:37. See also Luke 14:26.
6. Matthew 12:48–50. See also Mark 3:31–35.
7. Ephesians 6:1–3.
8. Anderson, *The Family and Pastoral Care*, 21–29, 41–49, 59–68.
9. Ibid., 17.
10. Ibid., 32.
11. Ibid., 57.

Chapter 3—A Values Crunch with the Younger Generation

1. Eva Leveton, *Adolescent Crisis: Family Counseling Approaches* (New York: Springer Publishing Company, 1984), 179–80.
2. John J. Mitchell, *The Adolescent Predicament* (Toronto: Holt, Rinehart and Winston of Canada, 1975).
3. Ibid., 1.
4. Lawrence Kohlberg, *The Philosophy of Moral Development* (New York: Harper and Row, 1981); *The Psychology of Moral Development* (New York: Harper and Row, 1983); and Lawrence Kohlberg and Thomas Lickona, *The Stages of Ethical Development from Childhood Through Old Age* (New York: Harper and Row, 1986).
5. Herbert Anderson, *The Family and Pastoral Care* (Philadelphia: Fortress Press, 1984), 38.
6. Ibid., 64.
7. Eda LeShan, *The Wonderful Crisis of Middle Age* (New York: David McKay Company, 1973), 135.
8. Frank Furstenburg, Jr. et al., "Family Communication and Contraceptive Use Among Sexually Active Adolescents," in *School-Age Pregnancy and Parenthood*, Jane Lancaster and Beatrix Hamburg, ed. (New York: Aldine De Gruyter, 1986), 240–41.
9. Catherine S. Chilman, "Some Psychosocial Aspects of Adolescent Sexual and Contraceptive Behaviors in a Changing American Society," in *School-Age Pregnancy*, Lancaster and Hamburg, ed., 199.
10. James Russell Lowell, "Once to Every Man and Nation."
11. LeShan, *The Wonderful Crisis*, 25.

Chapter 4—The Empty Nest Revisited

1. Robert Atchley, *Aging: Continuity and Change* (Belmont, Calif.: Wadsworth, 1987), cited in J. Jill Suitor and Karl Pillemer, "The Presence of Adult Children: A Source of Stress for Elderly Couples' Marriages?" *Journal of Marriage and the Family* 49 (November 1987): 718.
2. J. Jill Suitor and Karl Pillemer, "The Presence of Adult Children," 717.
3. Harold Ivan Smith, *Help for Parents of a Divorced Son or Daughter* (St. Louis: Concordia Publishing House, 1981), 9–12.
4. Ibid., 11.
5. Paul C. Glick and Sung-Ling Lin, "More Young Adults Are Living with Their Parents: Who Are They?" *Journal of Marriage and the Family* 48 (February 1987): 110.

Chapter 5—Caring for the Older Generation

1. Reuel Howe, *How to Stay Young While Growing Older* (Waco, Texas: Word Books, 1974), 121–22.
2. E. Brody, "The Aging and the Family," *The Annals of Political and Social Science* 438 (July 1978): 13–27; cited in Gordon Streib and Rubye W. Beck, "Older Families: A Decade Review," *Journal of Marriage and the Family* 42 (November 1980): 943.
3. Ethel Shanas, "Family-kin Networks and Aging in Cross-Cultural Perspective," *Journal of Marriage and the Family* 33 (August 1973): 263–90.
4. E.S. Johnson and B.I. Bursk, "Relationships between the Elderly and Their Adult Children," *The Gerontologist* 17 (February 1977) 90–96; cited in Gordon Streib and Rubye W. Beck, "Older Families," 939.

5. Eda LeShan, *The Wonderful Crisis of Middle Age* (New York: David McKay Company, 1973), 267–68.

6. J.M. Kreps, "Intergenerational Transfers and the Bureaucracy," *Family, Bureaucracy and the Elderly*, Ethel Shanas and Marvin Sussman, ed. (Durham: Duke University Press, 1977), 22.

7. Streib and Beck, "Older Families," 946.

8. Gary Lee, "Kinship in the Seventies: A Decade Review of Research and Theory," *Journal of Marriage and the Family*, 42 (November 1980): 925.

9. Ishmael O. Okraku, "Age and Attitudes Toward Multigenerational Residence, 1973 to 1983," *Journal of Gerontology*, 42 (1987): 280–87.

10. E.M. Brody, P.T. Johnson, and M.C. Fulcomer, "What Should Adult Children Do for Elderly Parents? Opinions and Preferences of Three Generations of Women," *Journal of Gerontology*, 39:736–46; cited in Ishmael Okraku, "Age and Attitudes," 281.

11. Okraku, "Age and Attitudes," 282.

12. Ibid., 286.

13. Brody, "The Aging and the Family," 20.

14. K.F. Smith and V.L. Bengston, "Positive Consequences of Institutionalization: Solidarity between Elderly Patients and Their Middle-Aged Children," *The Gerontologist* 19 (October 1979): 438–47; cited in Streib and Beck, "Older Families," 945.

15. William May, "Care of the Aging: A Clue to the American Character," an unpublished lecture given at the Chautauqua Institution, July 4, 1988.

16. Charles H. Mindel and Roosevelt Wright, Jr., "Satisfaction in Multigenerational Households," *Journal of Gerontology* 37 (July 1982): 484.

17. May, "Care of the Aging."

18. Ibid.

Chapter 6—Confronting the Death of the Older Generation

1. Eda LeShan, *The Wonderful Crisis of Middle Age* (New York: David McKay Company, 1973), 268.

2. Cited in Edward Myers, *When Parents Die: A Guide for Adults* (New York: Penguin Books, 1986), 90.

3. Dylan Thomas, "Do Not Go Gentle," *The Viking Book of Poetry of the English Speaking World* (New York: Viking Press, 1959), vol. 2, 1247.

4. Myers, *When Parents Die*, 46.

5. LeShan, *The Wonderful Crisis*, 275–76.

Bibliography

Anderson, Herbert. *The Family and Pastoral Care.* Philadelphia: Fortress Press, 1984.

Donnelly, Katherine F. *Recovering from the Loss of a Parent.* New York: Dodd, Mead and Company, 1987.

Filene, Peter. *Men in the Middle.* Englewood Cliffs: Prentice-Hall, 1981.

Hill, R. *Family Development in Three Generations.* Cambridge: Schenkman, 1970.

Hoge, Dean R. *Commitment on Campus.* Philadelphia: Westminster Press, 1974.

Howe, Reuel L. *How to Stay Younger While Growing Older.* Waco, Texas: Word Books, 1974.

Hulme, William E. *Mid-Life Crises,* Philadelphia: Westminster Press, 1980.

Kaplan, Louise J. *Adolescence: The Farewell to Childhood.* New York: Simon and Schuster, 1984.

Lancaster, Jane B. and Beatrix A. Hamburg, ed. *School-Age Pregnancy and Parenthood.* New York: Aldine De Gruyter, 1986.

LeShan, Eda. *The Wonderful Crisis of Middle Age.* New York: David McKay Co., 1973.

Leveton, Eva. *Adolescent Crisis: Family Counseling Approaches.* New York: Springer Publishing Co., 1984.

Matteson, David R. *Adolescence Today.* Homewood, Ill.: Dorsey Press, 1975.

Mitchell, John J. *The Adolescent Predicament.* Toronto: Holt, Rinehart and Winston of Canada, 1975.

Myers, Edward. *When Parents Die.* New York: Penguin Books, 1986.

Paine, Roger W. III. *We Never Had Any Trouble Before.* New York: Stein and Day, 1975.

Smith, Harold I. *Help for Parents of a Divorced Son or Daughter.* St. Louis: Concordia, 1981.

Stewart, Charles William. *The Minister as Family Counselor*. Nashville: Abingdon, 1979.

Troll, Lillian E. *Early and Middle Adulthood*. Monterey: Brooks/Cole Publishing Co., 1975.

Troll, L. E., S. J. Miller, and R. C. Atchley. *Families in Later Life*. Belmont, Calif.: Wadsworth Publishing Co., 1979.

Vedder, Clyde E. ed., *Problems of the Middle-Aged*. Springfield: Charles C. Thomas, 1965.

Vischer, A.L. *Old Age: Its Compensations and Rewards*. College Park, Md.: MacGrath, 1970.

Wynn, J.C. *The Family Therapist*. Old Tappan, N.J.: Revell, 1987.

———. *Family Therapy in Pastoral Ministry*. New York: Harper and Row, 1982.

Journals and Symposiums

Blieszner, R. and J.A. Mancini. "Enduring Ties: Older Adults' Parental Role and Responsibilities." *Family Relations* 36 (April 1987): 176–80.

Brody, E. "The Aging and the Family." *The Annals of Political and Social Science*. 438 (July 1978): 13–27.

Brody, E.M., P.J. Johnson, and M.C. Fulcomer. "What Should Adult Children Do for Elderly Parents? Opinions and Preferences of Three Generations of Women." *Journal of Gerontology* 39 (1984): 736–46.

Clemens, Andra, and Leland Axelson. "The Not-So-Empty Nest: The Return of the Fledgling Adult." *Family Relations* 34:259–64.

Feinauer, L.L. et al. "Family Issues in Multigenerational Households." *American Journal of Family Therapy* 15 (Spring 1987): 52–61.

Glick, Paul C., and Sung-Ling Lin. "More Young Adults Are Living with Their Parents: Who Are They?" *Journal of Marriage and the Family* 48 (February 1987): 107–12.

Johnson, E.S., and B.I. Bursk. "Relationships Between the Elderly and Their Adult Children." *The Gerontologist* 17 (February 1977): 90–96.

Kivett, Vira R. "Consanguinity and Kin Level: Their Relative Importance to the Helping Network of Older Adults." *Journal of Gerontology* 40 (March 1985): 2, 228–34.

Kreps, J.M. "Intergenerational Transfers and the Bureaucracy." In *Family, Bureaucracy and the Elderly*, edited by Ethel Shanas and Marvin Sussman. Durham: Duke University Press, 1977.

Lee, G.R. "Kinship in the Seventies: A Decade Review of Research and Theory." *Journal of Marriage and the Family* 42 (1980): 923–34.

Lesser, E.K., and J.J. Comet. "Help and Hindrance: Parents of Divorcing Children." *Journal of Marriage and Family Therapy* 13 (April 1987): 197–202.

Lopata, H.Z. "The Widowed Family Member." In *Transitions in Aging*, edited by N. Datan and N. Lohmann. New York: Academic Press, 1980.

Markides, Kyriakos S., Joanne S. Boldt, and Laura A. Ray. "Sources of Helping and Intergenerational Solidarity: A Three-Generational Study of Mexican Americans." *Journal of Gerontology* 41 (July 1986): 4, 506–11.

Mindel, Charles H. and Roosevelt Wright, Jr. "Satisfaction and Multigenerational Households." *Journal of Gerontology* 37 (July 1982): 483–89.

Okraku, Ishmael O. "Age and Attitudes Toward Multigenerational Residence, 1973–1983." *Journal of Gerontology* 42 (May 1987): 3, 280–87.

Seccombe, K. "Children: Their Impact on the Elderly in Declining Health." *Research on Aging* 9 (June 1987): 312–26.

Shanas, E. "Family-Kin Networks and Aging in Cross-Cultural Perspective." *Journal of Marriage and the Family* 35 (August 1973): 505–11.

Smith, K.F. and V.C. Bengtson. "Positive Congruences of Institutionalization: Solidarity Between Elderly Patients and Their Middle-Aged Children." *The Gerontologist* 19 (October 1979): 438–47.

Soldo, B.J. "The Living Arrangements of the Elderly in the Near Future." In *Aging: Social Change*, edited by S.B. Keisler, J.W. Morgan, and V.C. Oppenheimer. New York: Academic Press, 1981.

Streib, G.F. and R.W. Beck. "Older Families: A Decade Review." *Journal of Marriage and the Family* 42 (1980): 937–56.

Suitor, J. Jill and Karl Pillemer. "The Presence of Adult Children: A Source of Stress for Elderly Couples' Marriages." *Journal of Marriage and the Family* 49 (November 1987): 717–25.

Troll, L. "The Family in Later Life: A Decade Review." *Journal of Marriage and the Family* 33 (May 1971): 283–90.